The Art of Spiritual Warfare

Venatius Chukwudum Oforka

The Art of Spiritual Warfare

The Secret Weapons
Satan Can't Withstand

SOPHIA INSTITUTE PRESS
Manchester, New Hampshire

Sophia Institute Press
Box 5284, Manchester, NH 03108
1-800-888-9344

www.SophiaInstitute.com

Sophia Institute Press® is a registered trademark of Sophia Institute.

Library of Congress Cataloging-in-Publication Data

Names: Oforka, Venatius Chukwudum, author.
Title: The art of spiritual warfare : the secret weapons Satan can't
  withstand / Venatius Chukwudum Oforka.
Description: Manchester, New Hampshire : Sophia Institute Press, 2018. |
  Includes bibliographical references.
Identifiers: LCCN 2018013703 | ISBN 9781622825189 (pbk. : alk. paper)
Subjects: LCSH: Intercessory prayer—Christianity. | Spiritual warfare. |
  Catholic Church—Doctrines.
Classification: LCC BV215 .O355 2018 | DDC 235/.4—dc23 LC record available at https://lccn.loc.gov/2018013703

First printing

To all those who sincerely fight the battle of faith and endure all kinds of persecutions as a result, and to those who still tenaciously identify with the unadulterated teaching of Christ and courageously defend it

Bible Versions Used in This Book

Contents

Foreword

It takes a prophetic mind to diagnose the ills of a society, to detect its challenges and the "signs of the time" in order to perceive and pinpoint a possible way to a promising future. This responsibility of the prophet presupposes a courageous mind that can resist the enticements of political correctness, which conformingly relativizes and compromises to produce a glittering but noninspiring theology that ignores or explains away glaring facts in the lives of the suffering faithful and the yearnings of the militant Church of Christ.

The book in your hand is a treasure composed of the translated experience of a dedicated and wise pastor, whose enthusiasm and hard work have been a source of inspiration for many young men and women sincerely searching for meaning in life and the meaning of life by embracing the way of the Lord.

It is a contribution of an eagle-eyed, farseeing disciple in the Lord's vineyard, whose explanations and descriptions reflect his well-grounded experience in the ministry he describes — the fruit of a longtime service in the ministry of intercession! The inspiring examples and testimonies the author uses in his illustrations are very uplifting for the faith.

Tracing the ministry of intercession back to the early Church, the author demonstrates the paramount importance of the ministry of intercession in the salvific plan of God, and calling attention to the militant nature of the Church here on earth, he confronts the reader with a picture of a Church consisting also of the wounded and the vulnerable, a Church that is at war with a fierce enemy, but one that is nevertheless expertly equipped by an invincible victorious General, who is always present even in the hottest zones of the battlefield.

With a list of what he calls the arrows in the quiver of an intercessor, Father Oforka, as he is popularly known, reveals his vast experience as a pastor and a veteran on the side of the Lord in the spiritual battlefield. He demonstrates in this discourse the great treasure of the plurality of spirituality that reflects the unity in diversity of the one and holy Body of Christ, with its many parts, and elaborates how these different forms of spirituality can be applied in the ministry of intercession.

His prose makes the work very exciting and easy to read. He connects with the reader, helping him to discern and understand his role as a receiver and contributor in the framework of the history of man's salvation.

I recommend this book as a great help for those who desire to submit their lives to the Lord as intercessory ministers; as a guide for outsiders who want to have a deep and nuanced glance into the ministry of intercession; and as a help for discernment of spirits for all who directly or indirectly have to do with the mission of intercession.

Remigius Orjiukwu, Ph.D., Th.D.
Hirrlingen, Germany
June 9, 2017

Acknowledgments

I appreciate the contributions of the following priests: Christian Ikechukwu Amah, Dr. Philip Omenukwa, and Dr. Remigius Orjiukwu.

The Art of Spiritual Warfare

Prologue

"I urge that supplications, prayers, intercessions, and thanksgivings be made for all men, for kings and all who are in high positions, that we may lead a quiet and peaceable life, godly and respectful in every way" (1 Tim. 2:1–2). With this statement, Paul, a seasoned minister of the gospel and an experienced soldier in spiritual warfare, issues a clarion call for general intercessions and appeals to men and women of faith to embrace the ministry of intercession. This is a mission that is dear to the heart of the Lord, Christ Jesus, who is the only mediator between God and man (1 Tim. 2:5).

This appeal is based on Paul's knowledge that there are diabolical forces that work hard to see that we do not "lead a quiet and peaceable life, godly and respectful in every way." He was aware of the rage of the dragon, which failed in its bid to destroy "the woman and her child" but "went off to make war on the rest of her offspring, on those who keep the commandments of God and bear testimony to Jesus" (Rev. 12:17).

Paul knows therefore that we are involved in a spiritual warfare into which we were born and which shall continue until we die. It is for this reason that he announced in Ephesians 6:12: "For we are not contending against flesh and blood, but against the principalities, against the powers, against the world rulers of this present darkness, against the spiritual hosts of wickedness in the heavenly places."

This spiritual combat was foretold in Genesis 3:15 following the Fall of man: "I will put enmity between you and the woman, and between your seed and her seed; he shall bruise your head, and you shall bruise his heel." From this period in human history until now, a fierce spiritual battle has continued unbroken between the forces of good and the forces of evil, and man has been the apple of discord. Pope Leo XIII identified these two opposite forces as the Church of Jesus Christ on earth and those who desire from their heart to be united with it and the kingdom of Satan, in whose possession and control are all who follow the fatal example of their leader and of our first parents. He then said with a pontifical clarity: "At every period of time each has been in conflict with the other, with a variety and multiplicity of weapons, and of warfare, although not always with equal ardour and assault."[1]

A call to actively participate in this war is a call to get us involved in the shaping of events that affect our earthly and eternal destiny. This is because many of the events that take place in this world are not controlled solely by physical principles or forces but also by metaphysical principles or, better expressed, supernatural forces. Most of these events are determined first in the spiritual realm, whence they take their origin and authorization. This is why there can be prophecies and visions through which some upcoming events, when the Master deemed it necessary, could be revealed before they happened. This does not mean, however, that existence is founded on deterministic principles.

---

[1] Leo XIII, *On the Sect of the Freemasons* (London, Burns and Oates, 1884), pp. 3–4.

The spiritual forces that are also involved in determining the events that take place on the natural plane are not only positive or, if you like, godly or divine forces. Evil forces are also part of this spiritual web of powers that influence or determine most of the events that play out in this physical world. This is why Satan and his agents can sometimes rightly foretell the future—because they have some knowledge of what transpires in the spiritual realm. The spiritual assembly that was held in the book of Job, for instance, did not exclude these diabolical forces. Satan was present at this council and participated in the proceedings: "One day the angels came to present themselves before the Lord, and Satan also came with them" (Job 1:6, NIV). It is equally because the devil can appear in this council that he gets the opportunity to accuse people before God: "For the accuser of our brethren has been thrown down, who accuses them day and night before our God" (Rev. 12:10). He could also ask for and be granted permission by this council to do his evil deeds:[2]

> Then Satan answered the Lord, "Does Job fear God for nought? Hast thou not put a hedge about him and his house and all that he has, on every side? Thou hast blessed the work of his hands, and his possessions have increased in the land. But put forth thy hand now, and touch all that he has, and he will curse thee to thy face." And the Lord said to Satan, "Behold, all that he has is in your power; only upon himself do not put forth your hand." So Satan went forth from the presence of the Lord. (Job 1:9–12)

[2] The idea of "divine council" must be understood in a mystical rather than a physical sense. Spiritual beings do not live in time and space. Their gathering must therefore not be conceived in the ordinary sense of human gatherings.

The Art of Spiritual Warfare

Human beings are also part of the forces that determine how events turn out in nature. That is to say, they can participate in the supernatural councils and contribute in determining some of the events that take place both in the spiritual and in the physical world. This is not actually a privilege but a constitutive part of their nature. It is their right to be members of the supernatural council. They are not pure matter but a composite unit of matter and spirit. Their spiritual component qualifies them as spiritual beings with the power of transcendence. That is partly what it means to say that they are made in the image and likeness of God. This spiritual aspect offers them the opportunity, therefore, to transcend the physical plane and participate in events that take place in the spiritual domain. It is this spiritual aspect of man that makes him a combatant in the spiritual war declared in Genesis.

Prayer is the most legitimate and most accessible means to exploit this opportunity offered by the spiritual nature of human beings. Through prayer the human person frees himself from the encumbrances of the flesh to partake in events going on in the spiritual realm. When Jesus, during His ministry on earth, was emphasizing the importance of prayer, He was simply informing us of the need to exercise our rights of participating in the decisions that shape our lives here on earth and hereafter. That He made prayer the most important aspect of His ministry shows that He made Himself always available at the divine councils in order to be part of the decisions concerning His mission. This afforded Him the opportunity to checkmate the intrigues of the enemy in the on-going spiritual warfare.

Paul's call for prayer is a call for intercessions; an exhortation to establish intercession as a ministry to counter the accusations of the enemy in the divine council. Through intercessions, the petitions of believers find their way to diverse and numerous spiritual councils and relatively influence decisions in these councils, according to the nature of the issue in question and the intensity of the prayers. Intercessions stand in these councils, therefore, like the acts of an attorney defending a case before a judge: the success of an attorney in winning cases depends on the nature of the case he is handling, his sharp reasoning skill, and the power of his language, which draws from the knowledge of the principles of law. If his argument is so convincing, because it is supported by clear, authoritative principles, that his opponents cannot contradict him, he stands a greater chance of winning the case or of getting, at least, a mitigated sentence. Prayer works, more or less, along these lines.

When God said in Isaiah 1:18, "Come now, let us reason together," He was convoking a council to which His people Israel were invited. They were given the opportunity to argue their case before the divine council.

As an attorney can bring a case before a judge, so a human being can bring his petition before the divine Judge. The Judge will then listen to his arguments. If he convinces the Judge and successfully defends his submission against opposing attorneys, his petition will be answered.

This is how many great prophets and people of God obtained God's favor and destroyed the designs of the enemy, as evidenced in Sacred Scripture. A typical example of this is the petition of Moses when the people of Israel sinned and the anger of God burned fiercely against them.

Frustrated, God complained bitterly to Moses, His trusted servant and confidant, "How long will these people treat me with contempt? How long will they refuse to believe in me, in spite of all the signs I have performed among them?" (Num. 14:11,

NIV). In this formal complaint, God stated His case against the people of Israel. He established the ground that would justify His intended actions against them. The Lord's reasoning demonstrated His justice and consequently the justification of the verdict against Israel: "I will strike them down with a plague and destroy them, but I will make you [Moses] into a nation greater and stronger than they" (Num. 14:12, NIV).

The Lord set Moses apart from the impending destruction because the Lord would never destroy the just with the wicked, and He intended to raise a new people through him. But like a true intercessor, Moses was not a selfish man and therefore declined this attractive offer. He was ready to die for Israel. He understood that God might not have complained to him if His decision was absolute and that perhaps it could be appealed. Thus, he set out to wrestle with God, as Jacob his ancestor did with the angel of God, through putting up a defense for Israel.

Already, the unprovoked sin of the Israelites was strongly accusing them before the divine council. Their chances of being saved from the impending danger were slim. Nevertheless, a good spiritual attorney, a seasoned intercessor, can wriggle out a convincing defense to stop such a calamitous decision of the Master. That was what Moses did. He knew God. He understood some of the principles underlying divine operations and exploited them to save Israel.

Any human generation that lacks such great intercessors is doomed. Such a generation has no future and will have a troubled life because the enemy will freely carry out his wicked operations and oppressions. This is the reason St. Paul is calling for the ministry of intercession.

Through intercession, Christians also engage in the ongoing spiritual warfare and are able to frustrate the devil's onslaught against righteousness and those who bear testimony to the gospel of Christ. When there are no intercessors, the devil has a great opportunity to do evil, and the number of souls that are headed for damnation increases exponentially. This is why the clarion call to prayer is today more urgent than ever. There is obviously powerful satanic machinery operating with utmost decisiveness to restructure the world and erect its pillars on revolting abominations. Leo XIII would say, "The partisans of evil seem to be combining together, and to be struggling with united vehemence." Many powerful nations, for instance, seem to be leading humanity into destruction by the policies and laws they sponsor, and they surreptitiously force weaker nations to adopt the same diabolical principles that despise God and violate the ancient pact between humanity and its Maker: "Stand at the crossroads and look; ask for the ancient paths, ask where the good way is, and walk in it, and you will find rest for your souls. But you said, 'We will not walk in it.' I appointed watchmen over you and said, 'Listen to the sound of the trumpet!' But you said, 'We will not listen'" (Jer. 6:16–17, NIV).

The moral order has degenerated very badly in this generation, and disdain for God has grown intense. Our present condition is comparable to the time of the prophet Ezekiel, when God showed Ezekiel, in a vision, the abominations that were standing in the high places. He then told Ezekiel in utter displeasure and with a resolute disposition to pay back:

> Have you seen this, O son of man? Is it too slight a thing for the house of Judah to commit the abominations which they commit here, that they should fill the land with violence, and provoke me further to anger? Lo, they put the branch to their nose. Therefore, I will deal in wrath; my

eye will not spare, nor will I have pity; and though they
cry in my ears with a loud voice, I will not hear them.
(Ezek. 8:17–18, NIV)

Sadly, even the Church, the supposed moral conscience of
the world and the compass of right reasoning, sometimes seems
to be on the side of secularization. Some of her ministers tend to
be party to treachery against the Lord. Some of her leaders are
hardly faithful to the teachings of the apostles, and they seem
to have also abandoned the ancient path for worldly and carnal
interests, and promote revolt against the Lord and His teachings. A critical assessment of the status quo today will reveal
what Jesus experienced in the Temple of God in Jerusalem that
made Him drive away those who were doing business there: they
were buying and selling and making gains in the house of God.
They brought their cattle and birds into the temple of the Most
High, which muddied it with their droppings. Different catego-
ries of crimes were going on in the Temple of God in the name
of providing materials for sacrifices there. The true purpose for
the Temple became for the people just a ploy for them to pursue
their self-interests. In this way, they despised God and desecrated
His Temple. Thus, Jesus drove them out in a burning rage and
bellowed: "My house shall be called a house of prayer; but you
make it a den of robbers" (Matt. 21:13). Perhaps the case is no
different today in the Church of Christ, if not worse.

People with spiritual insight could easily perceive that the
stranglehold of the enemy, bemoaned by the psalmist, is once
again upon the Church:

The enemy has destroyed everything in the sanctuary!
Thy foes have roared in the midst of thy holy place; they
set up their own signs for signs. At the upper entrance

they hacked the wooden trellis with axes. And then all its carved wood they broke down with hatchets and hammers. They set thy sanctuary on fire; to the ground they desecrated the dwelling place of thy name. They said to themselves, "We will utterly subdue them"; they burned all the meeting places of God in the land. (Ps. 73:3–8)

There are many lost souls out there who do not even know that they are lost. There are many defenseless captives of the evil one, who suffer without respite. There are souls calling over the restless waves for light, without intervention. The Lord needs men and women who can send the light of the gospel to millions of hopeless souls in the cold and the dark and bring salvation through the ministry of intercession.

This bad state of affairs in our generation persists not only because "we are not contending against flesh and blood, but against principalities, against powers, against world rulers of this present darkness, against spiritual hosts of wickedness in the heavenly places" (Eph. 6:12), but also because many Christians have been hibernating spiritually for a very long time, though the spiritual war rages on.

There are strong signs that the divine patience may have reached its elastic limit. It is very probable that unless something is urgently done, the fury of God may overtake humanity. This will bring a terrible time of desolation. There will be great suffering and pain without respite, if this pending danger is not averted. It is sad, however, that the ears of this generation have grown too dull to heed divine warnings and listen to the voice of reason.

Who then shall go for the Lord on this errand of His? Who shall defend His sanctuary against foreign invasion and repair

His battered temple? Who shall rise in defense of the glory of the Lord? The one principal opportunity in the present predicament is recourse to intercession. Believers, who are still faithful to the Master and have not departed from the ancient path, are called upon to embrace the ministry of intercession and save our world from the desolation that is coming.

Through the ministry of intercession, men and women of faith are called to rise to the present occasion. They are equipped through this sacred ministry to confront and disband the furious army of the underworld and to divert souls from hell and people heaven to the glory of God. You are invited to join this sacred mission of spending passionate tears of supplication for lost and burdened souls and for our world lacerated by evil.

Chapter 1

A Clarion Call

Many Christians are not yet conscious of the spiritual war that is persistently raging in this world and especially in this present generation. They refuse to acknowledge that they are also involved in this war, and they are therefore complacent about the proliferation of evil in the world and the frequency with which God's name is ridiculed and His existence denied. Watching and analyzing with spiritual eyes the state of affairs in this generation reveals how furiously the devil promotes his cause in this warfare. He appears to be gaining ground in his mission to destroy humanity (or at least to further distort human destiny) and in his bitter opposition to the consummation of the kingdom of God on earth. It is for this reason that St. Peter the apostle warned: "Be sober, be watchful. Your adversary the devil prowls around like a roaring lion, seeking someone to devour" (1 Pet. 5:8). He is indeed committed to his cause.

Jesus Himself knew the nature of this spiritual battle very well and never stopped warning His disciples always to be awake and prepared for action. He urged them to "watch at all times, praying that you may have strength to escape all these things that will take place, and to stand before the Son of man" (Luke 21:36). He came from heaven to this dark world to engage in this long-declared battle as the Lord of the armies. He fought gallantly and conquered. In the most intense of His spiritual military actions, He exhorted and commanded His followers: "Watch and pray that you may not enter into temptation" (Matt. 26:41).

"Watching" and "praying" are the two basic actions Christians must undertake in order to survive evil days. Unless they watch and pray, they cannot hope to be victorious like their Master. This clarion call to "watch and pray" can be productively answered through the ministry of intercession.

The Ministry of Intercession

"Ministry" is the English translation of the Latin word *ministe-rium*, which means "service." In its sociological usage, it is applied to institutions or establishments that give aid and services to people. Its Christian understanding is defined by the manner in which Jesus exercised His mission among men: He "came not to be served but to serve, and to give His life as a ransom for many" (Matt. 20:28; cf. Mark 10:45; John 13:1–17). Christian ministries are thus selfless services rendered to people in the name of God for the salvation of souls and for the glory of God. Such services are driven by Christian love and for the sole purpose of higher values.

Intercession is the act of intervening between parties with a view to reconciling differences, or mediating in order to obtain favor from one of the parties for another. It is an interposing or entreaty on behalf of another person. Intercession in a Christian sense means, therefore, to stand between a needy soul and God, praying for God's mercy and gracious considerations. It is a vicarious supplication where one is given to agonize in prayer for the welfare of others.

As a ministry, intercession becomes an organized service in which people can individually or collectively send ceaseless prayers to the presence of God and entreat His help for distressed souls or situations. It acts as a form of spiritual legal aid for needy souls, which argues their cases in the divine council. In spiritual warfare, the ministry of intercession stands out as a manifest way of resisting the kingdom of darkness.

Jesus says, "All authority in heaven and on earth has been given to me. Go therefore and make disciples of all nations" (Matt. 28:18–19). Not everybody can be a literal missionary by going to the nations and spreading the good news of the kingdom or can engage in the formal ministry of spreading the gospel and saving souls. But one can become a missionary nevertheless through the ministry of intercession. There are so many places, for instance, where the gospel has been impeded or where some political policies have impaired the message of salvation. There are situations and conditions that need the urgent attention of heaven. These situations are such that one may not be able to reach and tackle them directly or even do anything directly to change them in order to save people from unnecessary suffering, break yokes, and bring restoration.

Believers can handle such problems through the ministry of intercession. One can become a missionary like St. Thérèse of the Child Jesus, who, without ever being a missionary in the conventional sense, brought many souls to God nonetheless through a hidden, simple life of prayer.

The salvation of souls is the Master's supreme concern. In Ezekiel 34:6, He complains: "My sheep were scattered, they wandered over all the mountains and on every high hill; my sheep were scattered over all the face of the earth, with none to search or seek for them." Commenting on this passage, Rob Wakefield notes: "There are lost sheep out there, people who need the Lord. Many of them don't even know they are lost, but they are out there in sin and their souls are in eternal danger. God cares about those sheep."[3]

Through the ministry of intercession, one participates actively in the redemption of the world, in seeking the lost sheep of the Master. A single person who opts to be an intercessor can make a great difference. People who really believe in the power of intercession, graced with a passion for souls, can greatly influence the divine council in favor of lost souls. Accordingly, the apostle James points out: "The prayer of a righteous man has great power in its effects" (James 5:16). Wakefield believes that if we were to be successful in our efforts to reach out to the lost and dying, it would be because we interceded.[4] Even souls gained through preaching and teaching of the word may not be retained without constant intercessions on their behalf. Intercession is a ministry that the Christian Church cannot do without.

Sometimes we need to go beyond our own problems and ourselves when we pray. We need to realize that we should pray for sinners, for backsliders, and for those who do not even know they need prayer or divine help. Praying for divine intervention in the lives of those who are at the brink of eternal damnation and the lives of the wretched of the earth is a very noble missionary service. Intercession is indeed a very profound way of extending the ministry of Jesus and saving souls. When Fulton J. Sheen was describing the profundity of passion for souls, he said: "What nobler work could there be than zeal for souls? What

---

[3] R. Wakefield, "A Passion for Souls" in *Higher Way Magazine* 93, no. 4.

[4] Ibid.

finer way to spend oneself and be spent than in drawing souls to the love of their Lord and their God?"[5]

Who wants to be an intercessor? Who cares for lost and perishing souls? Is there really someone who can go before the Lord and pray until tears flow for wretched souls? It is only this kind of prayer that can heal our wounded world and battered humanity. It takes hot tears of men and women passionately dying for souls to bring down the mercy of the Father on sinful men and women and on the world. It takes kneeling knees and upraised holy hands to draw down the power of God to heal, to break yokes, to restore, to console, and to bless. You are called to be a member of this noble class: an intercessor.

The Early Church and the Ministry of Intercession

The Church, the sacrament of salvation instituted by Christ, would not have survived the mortal persecutions that confronted her at a very tender age, and buoyantly flourished nonetheless, if the community of believers was prayerless and slumbering. The Church knew that her Master succeeded in establishing her because He was and remained a great intercessor, who never slept with two eyes closed. It was clear to the early Christians that the ministry of spreading the gospel, which was entrusted to them by the Lord, would not survive the heavy enemy artillery unless they could "lift up holy hands" (see 1 Tim. 2:8) to the heavenly sanctuary. They knew, therefore, the source of their strength and survival — intercession — and exploited it to the

---

[5] Fulton J. Sheen, *In the Fullness of Time: Christ-Centered Wisdom for the Third Millennium*, ed. Patricia A. Kossmann (Liguori, MS: Liguori/Triumph, 1999), p. 59.

full. Thus, before Pentecost, they were gathered in the upper room and "with one accord devoted themselves to prayer" (Acts 1:14). Because they had been saturated with passionate prayers during this time of waiting in the upper room, Pentecost became a great harvest of souls. Following the Pentecost experience, the apostles began the ministry of intercession in earnest, having been equipped with the anointing of the Holy Spirit.

The Acts of the Apostles helps us to appreciate the commitment of Jesus' early disciples to the ministry of intercession: "And they devoted themselves to the apostles' teaching and fellowship, to the breaking of bread and the prayers" (2:42). That means that they continued with the tradition that the Master had handed over to His apostles. Their central preoccupation revolved around three cardinal traditions: (1) the *teachings of the Lord* handed over to the apostles (the Word); (2) the *breaking of bread* (the Eucharist) which was the sacrament of unity, love, and the real presence of the Lord in their midst; and (3) *prayer* (the vehicle to attend the divine council). Through prayer they made themselves always present at the divine council, where they obtained the grace to expand the number of those who believed and to dismantle the roadblocks of the forces of darkness. Accordingly, "fear came upon every soul; and many wonders and signs were done through the apostles" (Acts 2:43). Through the ministry of intercession, they were able to move the hand that moves the universe, overthrow spiritual territorial powers, and hoist the emblem of the Master, marked with the blood of the Lamb and the power of the Resurrection. Because they maintained the tempo of the required commitment and did not relent in participating in the divine council through constant prayers and flooding heaven with tearful petitions for the salvation of souls, the Pentecost anointing continued to flow generously.

The power associated with the ministry of the early believers was made amazingly manifest after Peter and John were released by the Jewish authorities, following their arrest after the healing of the cripple at the Beautiful Gate. When they gave to the other disciples the report of their encounter with these authorities, who were resisting the power of God, they called upon the name of the Lord as a team of intercessors with one mind and one voice. They pulled their spiritual energies together and besieged the divine council: "And now, Lord, look upon their threats, and grant to thy servants to speak thy word with all boldness, while thou stretchest out thy hand to heal, and signs and wonders are performed through the name of thy holy servant Jesus" (Acts 4:29–30). Heaven responded with a blessed assurance. The evangelist Luke reported the consoling manifestation that confirmed the response of the divine council to their supplication: "And when they had prayed, the place in which they were gathered together was shaken; and they were all filled with the Holy Spirit and spoke the word of God with boldness" (Acts 4:31). Intercession was the glory of the early Church.

There are so many instances of the early Christians' commitment to the ministry of intercession and how this paved ways for the expansion of the Church and the harvest of souls. The story of the experience of Peter in prison will, however, suffice for these pieces of evidence that indicate the place of intercession in the life of the first-century believers.

After he had killed James the brother of John, Herod arrested Peter and put him in prison, intending also to kill him, "but earnest prayer for him was made to God by the Church" (Acts 12:5). The early Church was a praying Church. She had no other defensive or offensive weapon more effective than prayer. She knew that her advantage was "not by might, nor by power, but by [God's] Spirit"

(Zech. 4:6). Thus, while Peter was in prison, believers were in the divine council, wrestling with the intrigues of the accuser and asking the Supreme Judge for justice. They knew that it was "the time when kings go forth to battle" (1 Chron. 20:1) and not the time to slumber or to get drunk. They thus blew the war trumpet, gathered their army, and went to battle. The experience of Joshua, the successor of Moses, was then repeated with the apostles.

When Joshua gathered his army and marched out to take over Jericho, he looked up and saw a man standing in front of him with a drawn sword in his hand. He went up to him and asked, "Are you for us, or for our adversaries?" The man replied, "No; but as commander of the army of the Lord I have now come" (Josh. 5:13–14). That is to say, "If you are for the Lord, then I have come to lead you to battle. But if you are against the Lord, I am here to command the Lord's army against you."

Whenever the army of the Lord gathers for battle, the Lord always sends His angel to lead it to battle. It was this same experience that the disciples of the Lord had when their army filed out for battle against the spiritual forces personified in Herod. The Master sent His angel to lead them in battle even though they were not conscious of this like Joshua. As the commander of the army of the Lord, this angel went into the prison and released Peter unconditionally.

The intercession of believers has the power to obtain the services of heaven. The early Church was always in contact with heaven and always present in the divine council. This was how they made heaven always present in the world of their time.

Do we still wonder why the Church appears today more or less feeble and battered? Do we still wonder why demons can perch comfortably on the pews of our churches? Pope Paul VI sadly noted, "It is as if from some mysterious crack—no, it is not mysterious—from some crack, the smoke of Satan has entered the temple of God"[6] and has sometimes even infested its sanctuary. Believers have grown more and more ignorant of their roots and neglected their source of strength. They have grown too fat to go to war and too busy and distracted to appear in the divine council. The devil has used the enticements of the world as a lullaby and soothed them into drowsiness and stupor. When it is the time for kings to go to war, they stay at home like David (2 Sam. 11:1), romancing the devil. As a result of this situation, the devil has been enjoying a field day, wreaking havoc in the world and steadily dragging millions of souls to destruction. Would that the Church, the Body of Christ, might rediscover herself and exploit her powers once again. Would that believers might reclaim their dignity and measure up to their calling.

The Intercessor

Who is an intercessor? How can he be described? An intercessor loves God with an ardent passion and burns with zeal for His kingdom. For this reason, he adjudges the salvation of souls as his greatest concern and offers all for this purpose. Thus, he decides to act as an attorney who provides spiritual legal aid for needy souls. An intercessor makes the sacrifice of self for the welfare of others. He accepts sufferings for the well-being of others. He participates in the pains of Calvary so that others might be saved. He kneels and raises holy hands of supplication for others. The intercessor does not allow his personal needs to draw his attention from focusing his energy on the welfare of others. The well-being of the suffering and perishing souls is for

---

[6] Paul VI, Homily, June 29, 1972.

him very necessary and urgent. He goes through fire and storm to bring the power of God to bear on such souls. He has the eyes of an eagle and easily identifies the bond of oppression on people and situations that can breed or are already breeding sorrow and pain. He then readily bends his knees to intercede for these souls. His sacrifice is manifold and selfless.

An intercessor passes sleepless nights and days, storming heaven with tearful supplications. With fasting and deep sighs, he prevails on God to show His mercy on needy sinners. With a monastic asceticism, he engages in spiritual warfare, pulling down the spiritual walls of Jericho, stripping bare the forest of wickedness, and tearing asunder the bars of captivity. The intercessor is made of spiritual steel. He is tough and maintains his calm while he swims against the currents of opposing forces and resists the flaming darts of the enemy. He is fearless, courageous, and strong as he spits fire while wading through the enemy territory and crossing the battle lines. The intercessor is not discouraged when wounded. He does not doubt when the going gets tough. He does not count his losses but is always focused and determined to succeed. When he loses a battle, he moves on, focusing on winning the war. He possesses the spirit of St. Paul, the man who, in constantly difficult circumstances, like a wild ox, battered the bronze walls of principalities and powers of evil and opened the door of salvation to many. In 2 Cor. 11:23–27, Paul recounted his ordeals:

> Far more imprisonments, with countless beatings, and often near death. Five times I have received at the hands of the Jews the forty lashes less one. Three times I have been beaten with rods; once I was stoned. Three times I have been shipwrecked; a night and a day I have been adrift at sea; on frequent journeys, in danger from rivers,

danger from robbers, danger from my own people, danger from Gentiles, danger in the city, danger in the wilderness, danger at sea, danger from false brethren; in toil and hardship, through many a sleepless night, in hunger and thirst, often without food, in cold and exposure.

Despite all these sufferings, he was not discouraged but "fought the good fight, finished the race and kept the faith" (see 2 Tim. 4:7). He was a true soldier of the Cross who died at his post. Such should be the stuff of an intercessor. He should not relent, no matter the opposition.

An intercessor is a man of faith and keeps on holding the fort, even when it appears that all hope is lost. He keeps trusting, even when he does not understand. When he loses cases in the divine council, he surrenders to the absolute will of the Master, knowing that all things work for good for those who love God (Rom. 8:28). He understands that God can do all things but will not do all things.

An intercessor is one filled with the Holy Spirit and radiating the glory of God. He is the enemy number one of the devil, for he is a pronged bone in the devil's throat. The devil remembers him with horror, revulsion, fear, and bitter hate. He therefore gives him the tag "Very dangerous! Whenever and wherever possible shoot on sight." Whenever the knees of an intercessor touch the ground, with holy hands upraised, a cloud of destruction, like a battering ram, settles over satanic gatherings and habitations. Among the wicked he is known as "terror."

An intercessor stands the test of time. He is consistent, simple, urgent in his mission, sacrificing, selfless, insistent, and seasoned. He is faithful and true. He fears nothing, no matter the threat of danger. He loves and trusts the Master tenaciously. He is a close ally of the angels and the saints. He may not be really known among men, for he plays second fiddle. He is a humble lamb, convinced that he is the least among his brethren, yet he is considered great before God and spiritual beings. With such a personality, he carves a notch for himself in the heart of God. Such like him are the earthenware vessels that preserve the treasure for the redemption of the sinking world (see 2 Cor. 4:7). An intercessor is indeed the Lord's battle-ax, His weapon of war (see Jer. 51:20).

The Springboard of Intercession

The book of Genesis describes man as the image and likeness of God, while in 1 Corinthians 11:7 he is described as the image and glory of God. The impression of the Bible about man is therefore that he is the pride of God. In the sight of God, he is very dear and precious (see Isa. 43:4). For this reason, God loves him "with an everlasting love" (Jer. 31:3). God holds man so dear to His heart that He offered His only-begotten Son to pay his ransom, when man sold his soul to eternal damnation. His love for this creature, man, is too great to be fathomed.

Surely, God does not want to give up on man in spite of his many follies. It is not that by justice man does not deserve to be done away with. But God is intensely loving and merciful. His justice is bound intrinsically to His mercy. Thus, His boundless love, which is the source of His mercy, makes Him "weak" to deal with man according to the full force of His justice.

Jesus is the greatest expression of this divine love for man. His mission was to restore man and, through him, all creation. He was so consumed by this zeal that in spite of all that He had to undergo for the sake of man, Jesus was still ready to do more for him even after the Resurrection. He needed to provide him with some security before He ascended to the Father.

Consequently, when He met Peter and the other disciples at the lake of Tiberias after His Resurrection, He asked Peter that ominous and searching question: "Simon, son of John, do you love me more than these?" (John 21:15). Why did He put this question to Simon Peter? What did He imply by this question, and what answer did He expect from Peter? This question could be approached from different perspectives.

It could mean: "Do you love me more than your boat, net, and other fishing equipment, more than your career of catching fish?" Peter had, of course, gone back to his former fishing occupation after the death of Christ, perhaps out of disenchantment with the events he thought had marred the hope he and his colleagues had in Christ. He felt perhaps disillusioned and had thought that the story of the Son of Man was now relegated to mere history. He was probably trying to resuscitate his business and go on with his life after the scandal of the Cross.

But the Master found him once again. He still needed Him. He understood his limitations and weaknesses. He knew that his eyes were not yet open and his mind was still closed. It would take the power of the Holy Spirit to model him according to the mind of God and fashion him for the mission ahead. Jesus needed him for the pasturing of His sheep. He nonetheless needed to confirm his readiness for the mission Jesus had already prepared for him. Thus, He seems to have inquired: "Are you ready to give up everything, to abandon all hope of a successful fishing career, to give up a steady and lucrative job and reasonable comfort in order to give yourself forever to my service, to shepherd my flock, to the mission of netting souls instead of fishes?"

The Lord's question could also mean: "Do you love me more than the other disciples? Are you more passionate for souls than your colleagues? Are you ready to go the extra mile for the sake of my sheep more than the others would? Are you prepared to love most?" The Master had already intended to build His Church upon the leadership of this Rock that should define the faith and fate of the Church. If he must be the foundation, he must love more and be ready to sacrifice more than others. If he must be the general of the Lord's army, he must be more passionate about going to war than the rest of the soldiers.

The question could equally be interpreted in both these senses. Whichever is the case, the Master is trying to underscore the level of concern He has for His sheep, for the souls for which He died. He loves these souls and needed to secure a committed and diligent chief shepherd for them before going back to the Father. When Peter answered affirmatively, the Lord charged him, "Feed my lambs." That is to say, "Do not let my lambs starve."

The Lord repeated this question the second time but excluding the last phrase: "Simon, son of John, do you love me?" (John 21:16). The first question was meant specifically for Peter's position as the head of the shepherds, but this second one is addressed to him as one of the shepherds the Lord has appointed to lead and guard His flock. When Peter also expressed his love for the Master, the Lord commanded him, "Take care of my sheep." The Lord shifted from "my lamb" to "my sheep" here. This is not unintentional.

The Master made Peter realize here that his mission was beyond the mere feeding of the lambs. Lambs are young sheep. They do not need fodder. They feed from the milk of their mothers. The shepherd does not need to lead them to pasture. The major work of the shepherd toward them is to make sure they do not leave the confines of their pens or stray away from their mothers. But they will eventually become sheep and need more care and attention.

Thus, it seems the Lord was telling Peter, "Take care of my sheep and protect them from wild animals. Pasture them. Take them out and bring them into the pen safely. Bandage the wounded and lift up the weak on your shoulders. Seek the strayed and bring them home. Govern them with love and tender care. They are my sheep, and I love them. Do not let them get into trouble or eat unapproved fodder." It is little wonder, then, that the prophecy of Isaiah described the good shepherd thus: "He will feed His flock like a shepherd; he will gather the lambs in his arms; he will carry them in his bosom; and will gently lead those that are with young" (Isa. 40:11).

The Master's palpable concern for the welfare of His sheep is underscored by His asking Peter the same question for the third time. But why is He so solicitous for His sheep? Why is He so concerned for the future and eternal security of His lambs? Why is He so worried about what happens to His sheep when He is gone?

It is surely for the eternal welfare of these lambs and sheep that He became man and died infamously, like an accursed fellow on a tree. His mission on earth would be in vain if these lambs, the sheep, were eventually damned. His mission would not therefore be a successful one, if He did not lead them safely home to the kingdom of His Father. There are many wolves out there, seeking these lambs and sheep to devour. He cannot afford to see His mission thwarted, compromised, or unaccomplished after His Calvary ordeal. He needed trusted shepherds, who would lead His flock to drink from the fullness of the benefits of the Cross and the Resurrection.

We can understand from the foregoing how painful it is for the Master to lose any of this sheep. When He prayed in John 17, He assured the Father with a feeling of pride and fulfillment that He did not lose any of those entrusted to His care except for the one destined to be lost. Peter is therefore entrusted with the care of this flock of the Master that is so dear to Him. It is for him to oversee the welfare of the sheep. Peter vowed to do that and in so doing presumably canceled out his threefold denial of his Master. He carried out this mission with utmost dedication and sealed it with his martyrdom on an upturned cross.

There can be no true love for Jesus, therefore, without also an ardent love for His sheep. If there are lovers of Jesus, they too must commit their lives to the care of His sheep. Such people must be aflame with the zeal to save the lost sheep of the flock. They must possess the missionary spirit the Lord imparted on the apostles. We need more Simon Peters to die for the flock of the Master—not necessarily on the wooden upturned cross but on the gibbet of the knee, praying down grace and mercy for lost souls and for those in need. Anything that involves man's eternal salvation is God's special interest. It is for this reason that the ministry of intercession is absolutely necessary and urgent.

Another reason for the intercessory mission stems from the fact that what the mission of Christ achieved for humanity is an objective salvation. It adopted man formerly as a child of God. It made God's mercy accessible to him and empowered him to possess what is now his own as an adopted son. Prior to the death of Jesus on the Cross, man could not reclaim his dignified status because of the wages of sin. But now that his wages have been paid for and his chains consequently broken, he has been empowered to fight for his lost ground. The aim of the Master is to use the authority of His Cross and Resurrection to offer man a profound advantage over Satan and his evil works. He has accordingly provided him with the necessary paraphernalia for spiritual warfare and for his salvation. His act of salvation does not, however, plan to spoon-feed him but to make him a co-worker in the building of the kingdom of God, to fashion him into His battle-ax (cf. Jer. 51:20), and to use him to humble the Master's enemies. This is why it is written in the book of Isaiah: "With joy you will draw water from the wells of salvation" (12:3).

This precious well of salvation has been dug through the act of Jesus on the Cross. But the Master does not intend to draw the water for just anyone. He that is thirsty must go to the well personally to draw water to drink. Even when the road to the well is occupied by enemy forces, the Master would not draw the water for us. He has equipped us successfully to fight our way through and draw the water to drink. The prophet Obadiah also noted: "On mount Zion shall be deliverance and the people of Jacob shall possess their possessions" (Obad. 17 NIV). It is thus the duty of the house of Jacob now to take possession of its inheritance. The Master has authorized it, and it must take action. Each person must now work for his own salvation. This is what theologians call subjective salvation. Thus, we are saved objectively by the death and Resurrection of Christ, but each person must make this salvation his own through a subjective participation in the work of salvation. To fight our way through to the well of salvation, we must be praying Christians. Through the ministry of intercession we could help one another, especially the weak among us, to this well of salvation.

We must note that it is possible that the evil plunderer can still hijack our possessions. He can do that only when we give in and drink ourselves into a stupor with worldliness and carnality; when we grow faint and too busy to guard our hard-won possessions; when our souls are beset by the drought of prayer. We must not forget that he is still "a strong man" (Luke 11:21). But the death and Resurrection of Christ have made us stronger. This condition of strength can be actuated only through a positive response to life in Christ, and the ministry of intercession is a great means of achieving this.

The Urgency of Intercession

Jesus says that when a strong man fully armed guards his house, it is adequately secured. But when a stronger man comes, he binds him up and plunders him (Luke 11:21–22). Although the devil is "a strong man," Jesus is "a stronger man." Our alignment with Him has made us stronger, too, than the strong man, the devil. But the devil can become stronger, if we grant him the grace, and he will then be in the position to plunder us again and reclaim our possessions.

This is the simple reason he is still doing so much harm, as if to say that Christ died in vain. He is presently fighting like a wounded lion in the bid to regain his lost ground and despise the Master. He is snatching the inheritance of many and condemning many souls to hell. He is committed to build his kingdom of wickedness and malevolence. He is resolute on making the world ignorant of the knowledge of God and carefree about the consequences of sin. He wants men and women to believe in false doctrines and tenaciously hold on to false values, defend their wrong ways blindly but passionately, and live their lives accordingly. His mission is cunningly and slowly but steadily to dismantle the Christian values that used to be the foundation of very many nations. He has instituted a powerful machinery to accomplish this task. He is determined to make good his boast in Isaiah 14:13–14: "I will ascend to heaven; above the stars of God. I will set my throne on high; I will sit on the mount of assembly in the far north; I will ascend above the heights of the clouds; I will make myself like the Most High." He wants to be God. He is consequently destroying the knowledge of God among men and in the process building his throne in the world and spreading his false values.

We do not need a prophet to tell us that he is not being unsuccessful in his mission. It is obvious that wickedness has continued to rise, particularly in our generation. There is deafening worldliness and carnality. Righteousness is a scarce commodity. The devil has so successfully marketed defiance and shamelessness that people can today celebrate proudly in broad daylight evils that people could formerly perform only in the dark. They take great pride in affairs that were hitherto rightly considered shameful. They pride themselves as celebrities and mock those who oppose their ungodly lifestyles as phobic.

The intensity with which, in the name of democracy, freedom, and human rights, powerful nations are pressuring weaker nations to embrace lifestyles that have been previously justly considered atrocious shows how deep the tentacles of the evil plunderer have been planted in these big nations and how far he wants to spread his kingdom of falsehood. It is as if he were putting his seal on every nation, culture, and organization; and many are succumbing to his allurements.

Ideologies that oppose the authority of God and right reason are on the increase, especially in the Western world. There is much godlessness, and many do only what satisfies their pleasure. Morality has been redefined to mean merely what man finds good in his own sight, the so-called social morality (liberal ethics, liberation theology), whose foundation has no reference to God or the natural law. Children are robbed of their innocence because they are now taught from their childhood to consider adopting lifestyles that are abhorrent to God and basically contradict the law of nature. Man has pitched himself against nature and defiantly does things that are repulsive to its principles, forgetting that when one attacks nature, it must eventually hit back. He claims to work for the preservation of nature in order to save himself from what he has termed "climate change" or "global warming" but does not care about how much he pollutes the same nature morally and thus upsets many metaphysical principles of existence. He fails to understand that the moral order is part of the natural order. In his folly, man lacks the wisdom to appreciate the full meaning of the principle: "You reap what you sow." When Karl Jaspers forecast that man would eventually become the architect of his own destruction,[7] he was referring to the rising nuclear armament that began in the first half of the twentieth century. But the real self-destruction of humanity will be a result of jettisoning God from its affairs and the pollution of the moral order.

The most horrifying aspect of this predicament is that many Christian churches are caving in to the pressure of these satanic ideologies. They are compromising their moral teachings, distorting Scripture, and embracing the speed train of secularism. Even some ministers of God can no longer distinguish right from wrong, good from bad, out of either culpable confusion or regrettable mischief. They deface the message of the Master with impunity and preach distorted, lame messages to their congregations. In this situation, many more souls are getting lost with little hope of finding their way back home. The devil exploits the opportunity and keeps filling his barn with a bumper harvest of these lost souls. This is particularly the situation in places where the clergy neglect their pastoral duties and have no more time for the flocks entrusted to their care. The needy members of their flock are then pushed to seek help in wrong and forbidden places

---

[7] Karl Jaspers, *The Future of Mankind*, trans. E. B. Ashton (Chicago: University of Chicago Press, 1963), p. 3.

and, in the process, get entangled with demonic forces. This is the reason there is a sharp rise today in the number of Christians who devour horoscopes, visit mediums, practice sorcery, toy with magic, and engage in other such practices condemned by the Bible and the Christian faith. The frightening decline in faith has no doubt brought about the rapid growth of superstition.[8]

New Christian denominations have, nevertheless, continued to germinate like mushrooms, and many men and women take up pastoral works as priests, bishops, evangelists, deacons, deaconesses, elders, and so forth, especially in Africa, south of the Sahara, and in some other developing countries. Unfortunately, many of these new churches and messengers of the gospel are specialized gold diggers, who care for their wallets more than they care for the flock of the Master, while some are part of the demonic ploy to destroy, practicing witchcraft and sorcery in the name of evangelism and of pasturing the flock of Jesus.

Some Church leaders, if not many, have betrayed the Master and abandoned His flock to wolves and jackals. They have become unfortunate prisoners of the flesh and of the world, shackled in the dungeon of materialistic interests and squalid spirituality. Their materialistic penchant has made their ears too dull to hear the groaning of the distressed, enslaved sheep of their Master. Their minds are too coarse to be bothered by the threats and taunts of the war chants of the enemy. Their eyes are too dull to see the house of God on fire. They have grown too fat to go to war.

The prominence of the word of God is on a speedy decline in many churches. Many stretch out their necks endlessly for the nourishing and living word of God but receive little or nothing.

---

[8] Gabriele Amorth, *An Exorcist: More Stories* (San Francisco: Ignatius Press, 2000), p. 12.

They attend Masses and Church services famished, battered, wounded, dirty, smelly, hungry, broken, burdened, tearful, and faint, wishing and expecting to encounter the Lord, who heals, but they are unfortunately often sent home the way they came in or even worse, because the power of the pulpit has lost its smoking authority and the glory of God does not find a home anymore in many churches.

It is like the time of Ahab, the king of Israel, when the prophets of Baal filled the land of Judah and Israel; when false prophets, who were interested only in worldly gain, were readily available. It is like that period when the prophet Micaiah told Ahab, "I saw all Israel scattered upon the mountains, as sheep that have no shepherd; and the Lord said, 'These have no master; let each return to his home in peace'" (1 Kings 22:17).

For the ministers of the gospel in the early Church, the word of the Master was geared toward conversion and the building up of the Church. It was, for them, "the power of God that brings salvation to everyone who believes" (Rom. 1:16, NIV). They offered it to people as a lamp for their feet and a light on their path (cf. Ps. 119:105). But in this generation, many so-called ministers have turned it into a business enterprise. Some such ministers truncate the message of the Cross merely for personal aggrandizement. Other preachers twist the Bible to suit their personal opinions and desires, irrespective of the glaring message therein, which God intends for His people. Often, they tell people what they hanker for, what they want to hear, instead of what God wants them to understand, just for cheap popularity and other demeaning intentions.

The gospel of prosperity is therefore in vogue, and the word of God is made to revolve unfortunately around vanity, especially in developing countries. Preachers use undiluted sophistry to twist the untutored minds of the poor and needy, who follow as flies are drawn to overripe mangoes, because of what they deceitfully promise to offer. They preach so much about miracles and wonders, blowing them out of proportion, that people follow them with a mad rush, longing for what those preachers claim to offer, without any desire or ultimate search for eternal salvation.

These ministers spend much time teaching people about tithes and how the failure to pay tithes has been responsible for their life challenges. The poor, believing masses are told that the more they give, the more they will receive. Even if the people find it difficult to have one square meal a day, they are pressured to give so that they will receive. When the expected dividends of their tithes are not forthcoming, they are assured that their miracle is on the way. In this way, the coffers of "the man of God" grow fatter while his so-called flock starves. Yet Jesus strictly commanded His disciples, the ministers of the sacred treasure, when He sent them on this sacred mission, "Carry no purse, no bag" (Luke 10:4). But some of today's preachers opt for trucks. They simply do their own thing and prove only that they are religious frauds, who shrewdly blindfold their followers, hiding the fact that they are messengers from hell sent to twist the gospel of life into the gospel of guile and evil scheming. It is about a similar scenario that the prophet Micah sadly said: "Its heads give judgment for a bribe, its priests teach for hire, its prophets divine for money; yet they lean upon the Lord and say, 'Is not the Lord in the midst of us? No evil shall come upon us'" (3:11).

Many advertisements are made in the mass media and social media, especially on television and radio stations, by some so-called Christian groups, especially in developing countries, beckoning the public to come and be made rich or to be healed, and making other such spiritual offers. The Word and the entire ministry of the gospel are presented as if the minister is now preaching his own word and by his own authority and can dish out divine favors as he deems fit. Miracles, healing, signs and wonders, prophecies and visions, prosperity, and material favors dominate the ministry of these modern Christian groups and ministers. They have even faked miracles to confuse the ignorant. The salvation of souls becomes only a peripheral part of their mission, if at all.

This is how the word of God and the vision of the Church have been derailed, thereby deactivating the inherent power of the Word and the authority of the Church. Because of the disordered, lopsided, and impoverished sermons of many ministers today, the Church of Christ has degenerated to either a business center or a mere social institution. Of course, when the word of God is not preached with passionate conviction, without fear or favor, and selflessly too, it is as real as a mirage.

When, then, will the wealth of the Word be exploited once again so that the glory of God will rise upon His needy people? There are no more Moseses to lead the people of God out of their Egypts, no more Joshuas to pull down the walls of Jericho and lead them to possess their possessions. There are no more Elijahs to pray the fire down and cure the society of ignorance of the knowledge of God. There are no more Daniels to knock ceaselessly on the door of heaven to obtain heaven's attention. There are no more Isaiahs, Eziekels, Jeremiahs, and other faithful prophets to shape society with unadulterated messages from the holy sanctuary of God. Where is the Spirit of Pentecost? Where are the passion and the commitment of the apostles, the early Christians, and the saints?

Only a few Christians still talk about holiness, the righteousness that the Master preached. The leaders of the churches have continued to raise giant structures in the name of building houses for God, to spend millions of dollars on the renovation of churches and on social activities in their churches, while the enemy is very busy binding, devouring, and plundering the Church's hard-won patrimony. They give little pastoral attention to souls. The Church appears to be more or less a monument today, an ancient shell without content. It appears now to be just an institution with mere rituals, a mere social institution signifying nothing. It has become more bureaucratic than missionary.

Accordingly, people are sacramentally baptized but unconverted. Christians receive the sacrament of Confirmation without the Holy Spirit finding a home in them. Men and women who practice sorcery and witchcraft fill the churches and mock God, even in His holy sanctuary. Abominations are within the ranks of the hierarchies of the churches. People identify with or work for the churches with disordered ambitions and pursue them with astuteness and vehemence. While some are there to seek fame and amass wealth, some others are there to finetune their political ambitions or are there as agents of the devil, members of diabolical fraternities destroying churches from the inside; and yet others are there for vanity or reasons other than the service of God in spirit and in truth. For this reason, the word of God has continued to mock us, the so-called Christians: "This people draw near with their mouth and honor me with their lips, while their hearts are far from me" (Isa. 29:13).

This is an unfortunate situation. God is certainly disappointed. He is, no doubt, gazing at us, especially the churches, with sore displeasure. His creation is going awry again. A generation of evildoers is what He got in return for His goodness, and the churches seem to conspire with the world against Him. An impending doom, like the sword of Damocles, is consequently dangling menacingly over the head of this generation. God's rage is about to boil over. The avenging God may appear once again (cf. Ps. 94:1–2). For before the sins of Israel and Judah forced the glory of the Lord to depart His temple, the Lord said in His utter displeasure:

> Have you seen this, O son of man? Is it too slight a thing for the house of Judah to commit the abominations which they commit here, that they should fill the land with violence, and provoke me further to anger? Lo, they put the branch to their nose. Therefore, I will deal in wrath; my eye will not spare, nor will I have pity; and though they cry in my ears with a loud voice, I will not hear them. (Ezek. 8:17–18)

Is there any reason why God should not deal with this generation in accordance with this judgment on Israel and Judah? Sodom and Gomorrah were destroyed, supposedly without warning, essentially because of the sin of sodomy. Should this generation, then, be spared? Is this generation not more sophisticated in the evil that men do than Sodom and Gomorrah? Yet it has had the advantage of drinking from the gospel of Jesus, the Son of God. It has been taught the truth and offered diverse sacraments of salvation. What excuse would it present in its defense? There is none, and it has perhaps been marked for vengeance unless there is true conversion before the appointed time. The Lord will avenge His mocked glory and when the time comes, it will be like the episode in the book of Ezekiel:

> Now the glory of the God of Israel had gone up from the cherubim on which it rested to the threshold of the house; and He called to the man clothed in linen, who had the writing case at his side. And the Lord said to him, "Go

through the city, through Jerusalem, and put a mark upon the foreheads of the men who sigh and groan over all the abominations that are committed in it." And to the others He said in my hearing, "Pass through the city after him, and kill; your eye shall not spare, and you shall show no pity; slay old men outright, young men and maidens, little children and women, but touch no one upon whom is the mark. And begin at my sanctuary." So they began with the elders who were before the house. Then He said to them, "Defile the house, and fill the courts with the slain. Go forth." So they went forth, and killed in the city. (9:3–7)

If nothing is done to change the present condition of things before the anger of God is let loose, this generation may perish. The ministers of the gospel, the clergy who serve in the sanctuary, must equally note that when the time of retribution comes, it will begin in the sanctuary. They will be the first to drink the bitter chalice of God's rage and vengeance for consciously and persistently betraying their Master.

This could, however, be stopped. Moses intervened when Israel was marked out for destruction. But who would undertake the interventionist mission since the injunction "Feed my sheep" has become too obsolete for many Church ministers of this generation? They have relapsed into passivity and have become captives in the war in which they should be generals, commanding the army of the Lord. Who then can stop the impending danger?

It is in the face of this great despair that the power of intercession becomes the only hope. It provides the only ray of light on the unmarked dark path. The ministry of intercession takes, under this circumstance, a more urgent form than ever to appease the wrath of God. It is the only hope for surviving these evil days. The amazing power of intercession can save us from the impending peril. The intercessions of the saints have saved evil generations from the blazing anger of God in the past. The intercessions of the saints of this age, no matter how few they are, can save the present godless generation from the looming catastrophe for the sake of the sorrowful passion of the immolated Lamb. Only the praying knees, only the hot tears of supplication, only the power of an unrelenting appeal to heaven, can change this tide of doom. The need for intercessions is now more urgent than ever.

The power of intercession can be highly instrumental in praying the Church back to the ancient path, to her former glory. Most of the issues that have rattled the Church and rendered her lethargic are accomplished in the spiritual realm and can only be undone in the spiritual realm. The Lord therefore continues to ask: "Whom shall I send, and who will go for us?" (Isa. 6:8).

You can go for Him.

He is in dire need of your services. Just become, today, a kneeling Christian. You can help save souls for Christ. You can contribute to awakening a true revival in the Church.

This is a saying we can rely on: any problem that cannot be solved through prayer has no solution, assuming that human efforts have been exhausted. Prayer is a sturdy and most useful lever. Archimedes, the great physicist and engineer, once boasted: "Give me a place to stand and with a lever I will move the whole world."[9] With the lever of prayer and standing on the sanctuary of intercession, an intercessor can move any mountain and can turn the world around, for there is power on the knee.

---

[9]   Archimedes of Syracuse, *The Library of History of Diodorus Siculus, Fragments of Book XXVI*, trans. F. R. Walton, in Loeb Classical Library (1957), vol. XI.

Chapter 2

Returning to the Roots

We saw in the first chapter how the early Church responded to the instruction of the Master to "watch and pray." We have also tried to highlight their success as soldiers in the Lord's army, not only because they were committed to the injunctions of the Master but also because they were adequately equipped for the mission they were called to. Many centuries separate us from these seasoned men and women of God. It is therefore possible sometimes to forget and grow apart from our roots and from our mission as Christians.

A fable was told about an eagle who thought he was a chicken. When the eagle was very small, he fell from the safety of his nest. A chicken farmer found the eagle, brought him to the farm, and raised him in a chicken coop among his many chickens. The eagle grew up doing what chickens do, living like a chicken, and believing he was a chicken.

A naturalist came to the chicken farm to see if what he had heard about an eagle acting like a chicken was true. He knew that an eagle is the king of the sky. He was surprised to see the eagle strutting around the chicken coop, pecking at the ground, and acting very much like a chicken. The farmer explained to the naturalist that this bird was no longer an eagle. He was now a chicken because he had been trained to be a chicken and he believed that he was a chicken.

The naturalist knew there was more to this great bird than his actions showed as he "pretended" to be a chicken. He was born an eagle and had the heart of an eagle, and nothing could change that. The man lifted the eagle onto the fence surrounding the chicken coop and said, "Thou art an eagle. Stretch forth thy wings and fly." The eagle moved slightly, only to look at the man; then he glanced down at his home among the chickens in the chicken coop, where he was comfortable. He jumped off the fence and continued doing what chickens do. The farmer was satisfied. "I told you it was a chicken," he said.

The naturalist returned the next day and tried again to convince the farmer and the eagle that the eagle was born for something greater. He took the eagle to the top of the farmhouse and spoke to him: "Thou art an eagle. Thou dost belong to the sky and not to the earth. Stretch forth thy wings and fly." The large bird looked at the man and then down into the chicken coop. He jumped from the man's arm onto the roof of the farmhouse.

Knowing what eagles are really about, the naturalist asked the farmer to let him try one more time. He would return the next day and prove that this bird was an eagle. The farmer, convinced otherwise, said, "It is a chicken."

The naturalist returned the next morning to the chicken farm and took the eagle and the farmer some distance away to the foot of a high mountain. They could see neither the farm nor the chicken coop from this new setting. The man held the eagle on his arm and pointed high into the sky where the bright sun was beckoning above. He spoke: "Thou art an eagle! Thou dost belong to the sky and not to the earth. Stretch forth thy wings and fly." This time the eagle stared skyward into the bright sun, straightened his large body, and stretched his massive wings. His wings moved, slowly at first, then surely and powerfully. With the mighty screech of an eagle, he flew away.[10]

It is now time that we, the Church Militant, went back to our roots and rediscovered our true identity. Though we might have been living like chickens, we are not chickens. We are genetically eagles. We can reclaim our identity and soar higher into the heavens to participate in the divine council and repel the gathering storm of satanic invasion rather than remain comfortable on the earth, scratching the dirty ground with chickens, and searching for ants and worms.

Equipped to Conquer

The Church is the Body of Christ, instituted by Christ as a means of assisting souls to be saved. Christ Himself is the head of this Body, and all the baptized are the members. According to the tradition held by the Church, it was founded on what we call today "Good Friday" through the wounded side of Christ. It was founded to continue the mission of Christ, the hope of the sinking world and of battered humanity. It is for this reason that the Catholic Church describes the Church of Christ on earth as a militant Church. It should be a warring Church indeed, a Church at battle with all the spiritual dark forces in the heavenly places in order to liberate souls held captive and lead them to salvation.

The Church is constituted to resist the efforts of the enemy to distract many from the righteous path and conduct them away

---

[10] "Fable of the Eagle and the Chicken," in Jamie Glenn, *Walk Tall, You're A Daughter of God*, posted on Life Lessons, September 25, 2009, https://lifelessons4u.wordpress.com/tag/the-eagle-who-thought-he-was-a-chicken/.

from salvation, which Christ won for them with His blood. Its task is, no doubt, intimidating—fighting against forces that are invisible, more knowledgeable, wiser, more astute, more patient, more persevering, and, above all, more powerful. It is for this reason that the Lord did not send the early disciples into battle immediately after His Resurrection, nor at the time of His Ascension into heaven, but said to them: "Do not leave Jerusalem, but wait for the gift my Father promised" (Acts 1:4, NIV). He acknowledged the complex and challenging nature of the mission. As a result, He did not send the early Church into the battlefield before she was adequately equipped to engage her powerful and intelligent enemies in combat. The Church would become His battle-ax and continue the war against the dark forces. So, the Lord needed to vest the Church with the essential powers and authority through the anointing of the Holy Spirit to make her battle ready. With this configuration, the Master made the status of the Church dwarf the intimidating nature of the spiritual forces of darkness. The enemy could then be powerful, knowledgeable, wise, astute, patient, and persevering, but the empowerment of the Church through the Pentecost outpouring has made her more powerful, more knowledgeable, wiser, more astute, more patient, and more persevering than the evil one. Just a few of the principles of this authorization bequeathed to the Church by her Lord can help us understand how well the Master prepared her for the spiritual warfare:

> And I tell you, you are Peter, and on this rock I will build my Church, and the powers of death shall not prevail against it. (Matt. 16:18, NIV)

> For truly, I say to you, if you have faith as a grain of mustard seed, you will say to this mountain, "Move from here

to there," and it will move; and nothing will be impossible to you. (Matt. 17:20, NASB)

Truly, I say to you, whatever you bind on earth shall be bound in heaven, and whatever you loose on earth shall be loosed in heaven. Again, I say to you, if two of you agree on earth about anything they ask, it will be done for them by my Father in heaven. For where two or three are gathered in my name, there am I in the midst of them. (Matt. 18:18–20)

And Jesus answered them, "Truly, I say to you, if you have faith and never doubt, you will not only do what has been done to the fig tree, but even if you say to this mountain, 'Be taken up and cast into the sea,' it will be done. And whatever you ask in prayer, you will receive, if you have faith. (Matt. 21:21–22)

And Jesus came and said to them, "All authority in heaven and on earth has been given to me. Go therefore and make disciples of all nations, baptizing them in the name of the Father and of the Son and of the Holy Spirit." (Matt. 28:18–19)

And these signs will accompany those who believe: in my name they will cast out demons; they will speak in new tongues; they will pick up serpents, and if they drink any deadly thing, it will not hurt them; they will lay their hands on the sick, and they will recover. (Mark 16:17–18)

And He called the twelve together and gave them power and authority over all demons and to cure diseases, and

He sent them out to preach the kingdom of God and to heal. (Luke 9:1–2)

Behold, I have given you authority to tread upon serpents and scorpions, and over all the power of the enemy; and nothing shall hurt you. (Luke 10:19)

Truly, truly, I say to you, he who believes in me will also do the works that I do; and greater works than these will he do, because I go to the Father. Whatever you ask in my name, I will do it, that the Father may be glorified in the Son; if you ask anything in my name, I will do it. (John 14:12–14)

If you abide in me, and my words abide in you, ask whatever you will, and it shall be done for you. (John 15:7)

You did not choose me, but I chose you and appointed you that you should go and bear fruit and that your fruit should abide; so that whatever you ask the Father in my name, He may give it to you. (John 15:16)

Before His Ascension into heaven, the Lord made the apostles understand that they would need the baptism of the Holy Spirit to tap into these powers:

And while staying with them He charged them not to depart from Jerusalem, but to wait for the promise of the Father, which, He said, "you heard from me, for John baptized with water, but before many days you shall be baptized with the Holy Spirit." So when they had come together, they asked Him, "Lord, will you at this time restore the kingdom to Israel?" He said to them, "It is not for you to know times or seasons which the Father has fixed by His own authority. But you shall receive power when the Holy Spirit has come upon you; and you shall be my witnesses in Jerusalem and in all Judea and Samaria and to the end of the earth." (Acts 1:4–8)

And on Pentecost their hands were anointed for war and their arms prepared for battle (cf. Ps. 144:1). The powers inherited by the Church are obviously enormous. Now, all who are baptized into the death and Resurrection of Christ, as members of His sacred Body, have a share in this divine empowerment. These are, put in another way, the authority of those who believe in Christ Jesus.

It was on this wealth of authority that the early Church fed. In the early Church, great manifestations of the Holy Spirit were experienced. There were very many conversions. True testimonies of healing, miracles, and other divine manifestations followed the ministry of believers and confirmed that Christ was the head of His Body, the Church. They shed their blood and did not shrink from the threat of death in their determination to accomplish and defend the mission the Master entrusted to them: "Go therefore and make disciples of all nations … teaching them to observe all that I have commanded you" (Matt. 28:19–20). They were overwhelmingly persecuted but were never intimidated. The storm they experienced was very tough, but their light kept on burning. They never gave up. The more they were persecuted, the more passionate their zest for the missionary mandate became. They drank copiously from the well of their authority as believers and thrived as the Master expected.

When one would think that these early believers would break, they prayed the more for more infilling with the power of the Holy Spirit. They asked God for the confirmation of His word with signs and wonders. God answered their prayers generously.

He blessed their efforts and perseverance abundantly. These holy men and women, who planted the seed of the gospel with their sweat and blood, took over many nations that were previously completely pagan territories and succeeded in incarnating the gospel in these cultures. So many of them had language and cultural barriers, religious and climatic oppositions, yet they were able to capture territories for the Master. The phenomena of those days proved the word of God to be truly "living and active, sharper than any two-edged sword" (Heb. 4:12). The powers given to the Church were adequately utilized by the believers of these early centuries, and the result was phenomenal.

The events of this early period were not simply because the Church was at her nascent stage and needed to be established with such evidence of great manifestations, as some theologians would like to argue. If that were the case, then the power of the word of God was limited to that period, and the authority of the Church to conquer evil was not intended to go beyond this early period. This would mean that from the onset, the life span of the Church was meant to be brief. This would have been unfortunate. If the word of God had come to us lame, could there have been any ground for us to call confidently upon the name of God or even believe in Him? Should we have had any reason to abandon the religion of our ancestors for the Christian religion? No one should therefore take God for a liar. To accept a feeble theological apology in defense of the Christians' failures to exploit the power in the authority bequeathed the Church would be escapist. The achievements of these fiery men and women of God were rather because of their conviction about the message they received, their commitment to disseminating it, their determination to live in accordance with its dictates, their readiness to feed the sheep of the Master according to the Master's stipulations, and their consistent engagement in the spiritual battle aimed at populating heaven. They took Jesus and His injunctions very seriously. They were ready to do anything legitimate, sacrifice anything, for the mission they received on trust as the truest of values.

The Christians of today have therefore so much to learn from these brethren of theirs, if they are to thrive in this generation. Since it is essentially the same Church that lives on today, the same effect will be produced if the actions the early Christians took are taken today. The past challenges the present. It is time that the Church in this generation rediscovers the secrets of the success of these men and women who came before and now, marked with the mark of victory, rest in glory. If our generation must be won for God, and if the Church must still be relevant today as the moral conscience of the world, the Church must repossess the intense zeal of the early Church, her audacious courage, her uncompromising faith, and her unflinching fidelity; she must master above all the art of intercession. This means that the Church must return to her roots. Christians must rediscover their origin and true identity.

When we reclaim the wisdom of the early Church, the missionary fire will be lit again and the flame of conversions and re-conversions will burn brightly. The Church is never meant to be a cold room, but it appears presently that many flies are buzzing in and around the churches comfortably because of the coldness of decay in them. Of course, it is only on a cold stove that flies can perch. When the zeal of the apostles and the first-century Christians fully resurrects, every fly must either die or take flight.

The Logic of Intercession

"And I sought for a man among them who should build up the wall and stand in the breach before me for the land that I should not destroy it; but I found none. Therefore, I have poured out my indignation upon them; I have consumed them with the fire of my wrath; their way have I requited upon their heads, says the Lord God" (Ezek. 22:30–31). Ezekiel prophesied at a time when there was great moral decadence in Israel. There was pervading godlessness and anarchy. People shed blood with reckless abandon. God described them in the prophecy of Ezekiel as "a roaring lion tearing its prey" and as "killing for an unjust gain." The priests were so abysmally debased that they too were doing violence to the law of God and profaning holy things without any qualms. They could no longer distinguish between the holy and the profane, the clean and the unclean (cf. Ezek. 22:23–29). God was appalled to see this happening in the land and decided accordingly to allow the destruction to overtake them, as their sins necessitated. For the wages of sin is death (Rom. 6:23), and therefore the soul that sins shall die (Ezek. 18:4).

Yet God wished He had reasons not to follow this course of justice and let the consequences of sin consume them. He desired to have grounds to justify His refusal to let this happen. This is because His plans for His people are not to harm them but rather to give them hope and a future (Jer. 29:11). It is for this reason that He looked for a man who would build up the wall, stand in the gap on behalf of sinners, and stop Him from destroying them (cf. Ezek. 22:30). He simply wished someone would intercede on their behalf and save the situation, as Moses did for Israel.

Why did God not wish to let sinners reap what they planted?

Why was He looking for an intercessor to build a wall and give Him reasons that would offset the balance of justice and bring the impending tragedy to an end?

He is God, and His strongest attribute is mercy. His mercies endure forever; they are new every morning, and great is His faithfulness (see Lam. 3:23). Although He is a just God, who does not spare iniquity, He does not relish the destruction of His own creation. Although His eyes are too holy to behold wickedness (see Hab. 1:13), He does not want a sinner to die (see Ezek. 18:30). He does not enjoy the woes and sufferings of those He created in His own image and likeness. He loves them with an everlasting love and is faithful to this commitment (Jer. 31:3). He is more disposed to give life than death. It is painful for God to permit destruction. Sometimes He grieves that He made such decisions: "I will never again curse the ground because of man, for the imagination of man's heart is evil from his youth; neither will I ever again destroy every living creature as I have done" (Gen. 8:21). He would thus do all that is necessary or seek all possible interventions to do otherwise, when there is a justifiable demand to pay the wages of sin. He does not want a sinner to die but rather to turn back from his evil ways and live (see Ezek. 18:23). Yet in His justice, He treats each man according to his deeds (cf. Job 34:11; Rom. 2:6).

In this seeming divine impasse, an intervention by an intercessor through prayer will be most cherished by the Lord. That is why He looked for someone who would build a wall before Him on behalf of sinners and stop the imminent evil. He was only seeking someone who would plead for sinners and neutralize the chalice of retribution, which stands before the divine council, demanding justice. The Master wanted somebody to blunt the shafts of His retributive justice against evildoers and sharpen the edges of His mercy. He needed something to hang on as an excuse to terminate the course of painful retributive justice while remaining a just God. If God must not allow the dialectics of sin or wickedness to be logically concluded, there must be a forceful and justified reason. Because He is not arbitrary in His acts, He cannot just stop it. An intercessor can provide Him with this much-needed reason to sheath the sword.

God is therefore looking for somebody, a wall builder; somebody, who can prevent calamities and avert disasters through importunate tears of supplication. Such wall builders attend the divine council and, like spiritual attorneys, passionately argue their cases in order to achieve their purpose. This was what Moses, the servant of God, did for Israel throughout the time he led them as a people of God. His soulful intercessions contributed to the realization of God's promise to His servant Abraham.

When the people of Israel sinned against God in Exodus 32, God could have wiped them off the face of the earth but for the intervention of Moses. This people committed idolatry, which God considers the most abhorrent of sins. What made this sin very grievous and damaging was the fact that they had just crossed the Red Sea and sung the might and power of God: "Who is like thee, O Lord, among the gods? Who is like thee, majestic in holiness, terrible in glorious deeds, doing wonders?" (Exod. 15:11). They experienced the manifestations of God in Egypt and saw at their point of leaving Egypt how He defended them against the swords of the Egyptians. It was very clear to them how He stood between them and the Egyptians as a pillar of fire and a pillar of cloud to protect them from the fierce Egyptian army that pursued them. He gave them light, but with a thick cloud obscured the view of the Egyptian military troops. He provided them with manna daily and water from the rock. They had abundantly experienced His power as God. How could they now mold a calf and bow down to it and proclaim: "These are your gods, O Israel, who brought you out of the land of Egypt!" (Exod. 32:8)? It had taken only a few days while Moses, who was receiving the Ten Commandments from God on Mount Sinai, was absent from the camp. They had no reason whatsoever to commit this grievous sin. This was why the anger of God burned so fiercely that He said to Moses: "I have seen this people, and behold, it is a stiff-necked people; now, therefore, let me alone, that my wrath may burn hot against them and I may consume them; but of you I will make a great nation" (Exod. 32:9–10).

This is a divine decision. Israel had sinned gravely, and God is justified in His anger and decision to wipe them off the face of the earth. But the curious questions here are: Why did He tell Moses about it? Why did He complain to him? Why did He not do it without the knowledge of Moses? Why did He seek permission from His servant Moses and say, "Now, therefore let me alone, that my wrath may burn hot against them and I may consume them"?

Moses was acting as the bridge between God and His people. That was an office that God called him to when He appeared to him in the form of a burning bush. He therefore respects both Moses as His faithful servant and His office of mediation between Him and His people. He informed Moses and asked for his permission out of respect for him and for his office. He needed to go through Moses officially to get to His people. And insofar as Moses remained in the gap, God might not achieve His threat.[11] Secondly, though He was very angry and bound, according to the principles of justice, to deal with this stubborn people, He wished this could be prevented. He wanted something to use as an adequate alibi to put off His threat. He actually wanted Moses to intervene so that He could lean on Moses as the reason to

---

[11] Note that our language to speak about God can only be anthropomorphic. There is no human language that can be adequate to explain the logic of divine actions.

nullify the logical implementation of His divine justice without being an unjust God.

This passage also reveals to us a further divine secret. There are cases in the divine realm that are relatively decided and could be changed, if right actions are taken. This is one of them, and that is the reason God sought the permission of Moses. Some others are absolutely determined and cannot be changed, no matter what. In such cases, God may act without informing His prophets. That was what happened when Israel worshiped Baal at Peor and had forbidden sexual relations with the women of Moab. This precipitated a plague that consumed twenty-four thousand people before the anger of the Lord could be sated. He did not inform Moses about this before He struck.

We can now begin to visualize, even if in a very limited measure, how the ministry of intercession works. God needs it to save souls. The early Church understood this secret and gave herself to intercessions. That was why heaven was always accessible to them: God needed their prayers to accomplish His purpose of increasing the number of those who were to be saved.

An intercessor has a great worth before the Master. He respects him, for his position is an exalted one. God needs intercessors for some of the decisions He makes. He gladly leans on them to save souls, which otherwise would have been lost. In such matters that are conditionally willed by God, He would expect intercessors to stand in the gap. It is for this reason that He complained: "But when I look there is no one; among these there is no counselor who, when I ask, gives an answer" (Isa. 41:28). This much-needed counselor is the intercessor, the spiritual attorney in the divine council. He is the person who provides defense for the accused. If there were counselors, who stand ready to supply the necessary answers and argue the cases of helpless defendants in the divine council, a lot of tragedies would be prevented, and more souls saved. But when there are no such advocates, the reverse might be the case.

When God told Moses, "Now leave me alone so that my anger may burn against them," the fate of Israel was lying relatively in the hands of Moses. If he did not resist God, God would have made good His threat. Intercessors enjoy the same consideration and respect. God does not spurn reasonable arguments when they are presented in the proceedings of the divine council. Rather, He expects them from us and would be surprised if they did not come. He even challenges us to do so: "Put me in remembrance, let us argue together; set forth your case, that you may be proved right" (Isa. 43:26). We must therefore go back to our roots and repossess the right of attending the divine council through the ministry of intercession.

A Spiritual Attorney before the Divine Council

As a seasoned spiritual attorney, Moses immediately understood what was at stake when the Lord complained to him and was ready to destroy. He knew that he, Moses, had the life and death of Israel in his hand at that moment because God had played the ball into his court and was waiting for him to give answer. God's further actions would depend on the response of Moses. But Moses had experienced God enough to understand some of the principles of His operations. So, he knew what to do and went to work immediately. Accordingly, he appealed God's decision with the following argument:

> O Lord, why does thy wrath burn hot against thy people, whom thou hast brought forth out of the land of Egypt

with great power and with a mighty hand? Why should the Egyptians say, "With evil intent did He bring them forth, to slay them in the mountains, and to consume them from the face of the earth"? Turn from thy fierce wrath and repent of this evil against thy people. Remember Abraham, Isaac, and Israel, thy servants, to whom thou didst swear by thine own self, and didst say to them, "I will multiply your descendants as the stars of heaven, and all this land that I have promised I will give to your descendants, and they shall inherit it forever." (Exod. 32:11–13)

Another version of this argument in the book of Numbers states:

But Moses said to the Lord, "Then the Egyptians will hear of it, for thou didst bring up this people in thy might from among them, and they will tell the inhabitants of this land. They have heard that thou, O Lord, art in the midst of this people; for thou, O Lord, art seen face to face, and thy cloud stands over them and thou goest before them, in a pillar of cloud by day and in a pillar of fire by night. Now if thou dost kill this people as one man, then the nations who have heard thy fame will say, 'Because the Lord was not able to bring this people into the land which He swore to give to them, therefore He has slain them in the wilderness.'" (Num. 14:13–16)

Good logic! The argument is as persuasive as it is incisive. It is an intelligent presentation intended to move God to "sobriety" and to activate His mercy by a subtle appeal to His sensitivity to the dignity and integrity of His holy name. Moses knew that the Israelites had no excuse to have done what they did. He understood that the case was a very bad one and offered no good ground for appeal. He intelligently noticed, however, that he could receive mercy for Israel, if he could move God to defend the glory of His name instead of directly appealing to Him to show Israel His mercy. He was aware that God would never compromise the glory of His name but, on the contrary, would sacrifice anything to defend His name from being ridiculed among His enemies. He therefore decided to exploit this "weakness" of God. He knew that this would be an indirect way of saving Israel from the burning anger of God. And he was right. He touched God where He could not resist changing or at least amending His decision.

To buttress his point, Moses invoked the promise God made of old to Abraham. He reminded him that He would not set His word aside; otherwise He would not be a faithful God. This is where we see the power of reminding God of His utterances, His promises, in the intercessory mission, as we shall discuss later. God is committed to His word and would respect the word of His lips. For "God is not man, that He should lie, or a son of man, that He should repent. Has He said, and will He not do it? Or has He spoken, and will He not fulfil it?" (Num. 23:19). Moses knew these facts and exploited them. As he presented his case like an attorney, the heavenly Judge listened with interest. He reasoned along with him and was convinced that Moses was right. He then "repented of the evil which He thought to do to His people" (Exod. 32:14).

Moses' appeal could not, however, entirely save the people of Israel from the punishment due to their sin of idolatry, but it was enough to mitigate it, for God replied to him: "I have pardoned, according to your word; but truly, as I live, and as all the earth shall be filled with the glory of the Lord, none of the men who have seen my glory and my signs which I wrought in Egypt and in the wilderness, and yet have put me to the proof these ten times and have not hearkened to my voice, shall see the land which I swore to give to their fathers; and none of those who despised me shall see it" (Num. 14:20–23). It is so in the ministry of intercession. Sometimes the intercessor wins a case completely; sometimes he succeeds in mitigating an intended disaster or obtaining just part of his request. Sometimes, too, he "loses" a case and must then surrender to the absolute will of the Master.

It is always the joy of an intercessor to experience a positive response of heaven to his appeal. If Moses had not stood at the gap and built a bridge of mediation, the story would have been different. At the success of every intercessory move, the intercessor rejoices that a bad situation has been fixed and that the evil one has been denied an opportunity to gloat over God and His people.

Intercession can be very demanding and strenuous. There are indeed many cases and people that need a strenuous prayer fight to save them. The arduous nature of this task notwithstanding, God is never happy when there is nobody to intercede. This is further highlighted by the prophet Isaiah: "The Lord saw it, and it displeased him that there was no justice. He saw that there was no man, and wondered that there was no one to intervene" (Isa. 59:15–16). God saw injustice and did not like it. He was ready to redress it but there was nobody stirring His hand for action. He wanted somebody to do something. An intercessor was needed to argue this case of injustice in the divine council in order that the oppressed would experience justice. But He saw no one to bring the case before the divine council. One might think that the statement above weakens God's omnipotence:

Why must God want us to do something before He could step in, as if He depends on man to achieve His purposes? Because we are part of the spiritual web, we have the right and the duty to engage in positive spiritual efforts that cooperate with and complement His acts to save. It must be clear to us that God no longer creates *ex nihilo* (out of nothing). He can still create out of nothing, but He may not create out of nothing anymore. In this case He achieves some of His purposes from the raw materials of prayer we pour in, depending on the nature of the cases. He does not do things arbitrarily. His actions must be justified. He needs our prayers sometimes to justify His actions to save us. This was true about God and His people in the Old Testament, and it is still true. The sacrifice of Jesus may not therefore help us without our cooperation.

It is possible that God may not approve of a situation but only allow it to happen. That is to say, He might be neutral in relation to a situation. Here, the case is one of the open-ended situations in life. The supreme Judge has given no judgment about them because perhaps defensive arguments have not been presented for consideration in the divine council. A good spiritual attorney can bring about a positive result in this situation by bringing them forward in the divine council and arguing like Moses for a favorable decision. The devil's advocate can equally make it go the other way, when there is no intercessor to intervene and stand in the gap. This is the way things can go wrong, and we call them the will of God when we could have prevented them. Such situations give real concern to God, but because no one conditions His conditional will, the enemy might take the liberty to condition it to his malevolent advantage.

That is why God is appalled that there is no one to intervene. He is disappointed that no one is doing anything serious for all the injustices that are going on in the land. He is disenchanted with the passivity of His Christians because He "looked, but there was no one to help, [and] was appalled that no one gave support" (Isa. 63:5, NIV). If there were people who were giving support, the situation of the Church would not have become so dismal today. If there were people giving help, our world would not be so mired in the mud of godlessness. Thus, the Lord utters distressingly: "His watchmen are blind; they are all without knowledge; they are all dumb dogs; they cannot bark; dreaming, lying down, loving to slumber. The dogs have a mighty appetite; they never have enough. The shepherds also have no understanding; they have all turned to their own way, each to his own gain, one and all" (Isa. 56:10–11).

The example of Moses acting as the attorney of the people of God explains how intercessors should appear before the divine council to present their own cases. One does not need to hold a special office in the Church to do this. Anyone can be an intercessor. It is the ministry of all the baptized. Daniel was simply a Jew who loved God and performed his duty of presenting the case of Israel in exile before the divine council. His passion for the service of God began as a young man. He made himself available for God's use, and God used him powerfully as His weapon of war. So, let Daniels gather together wherever they find themselves and give their knees to intercession. They could also go into their private rooms individually and groan for lost souls. The zeal of God is still very strong to save but needs the cooperation of men, intercessors, spiritual attorneys, taking their place in the divine council like Moses and Daniel. That was the life of the early Church: we must trace our steps back to this root.

Chapter 3

Preparing for War

After a long fruitful service in the mission the Lord gave him and after diverse encounters with the forces of darkness in the battle of faith, St. Paul informs believers of how they should be equipped for the spiritual battle in order to survive the spiritual warfare:

> Finally, be strong in the Lord and in His mighty power. Put on the full armor of God, so that you can take your stand against the devil's schemes. For our struggle is not against flesh and blood, but against the rulers, against the authorities, against the powers of this dark world and against the spiritual forces of evil in the heavenly realms. Therefore, put on the full armor of God, so that when the day of evil comes, you may be able to stand your ground, and after you have done everything, to stand. Stand firm then, with the belt of truth buckled around your waist, with the breastplate of righteousness in place, and with your feet fitted with the readiness that comes from the gospel of peace. In addition to all this, take up the shield of faith, with which you can extinguish all the flaming arrows of the evil one. Take the helmet of salvation and the sword of the Spirit, which is the word of God. And

pray in the Spirit on all occasions with all kinds of prayers
and requests. (Eph. 6:10–18, NIV)

With these instructions he prepares Christians for the long-ex-
isting spiritual warfare. His first exhortation is: "Be strong in the
Lord and in His mighty power." This makes it clear to all the
members of the Lord's army that it is only through the strength
and power of God that they can successfully engage in this spiritual battle. For apart from God they can do nothing (cf. John
15:5). Jesus made it abundantly clear to His disciples that "it is
the spirit that gives life, the flesh is of no avail" (John 6:63). Thus,
whoever wishes to enter into the army of the Lord must enter into
a sincere and consistent relationship with God. It is only in this
way that he can "be strong in the Lord and in His mighty power."

"Put on the full armor of God": this is a command and not
merely advice. If a Christian wants to outmaneuver the devil, it
has to be the whole armor of God or nothing. Just as in physical
wars, there is no taking of chances in spiritual warfare. This is,
however, more emphasized in spiritual battles because the adversaries in these battles are not corporeal beings but spiritual
forces that are more intelligent and swifter in relation to bare
human strength. They are thus very dangerous and can very
easily rout out their human foes without the protection of the
whole armor of God. It is for this reason that Paul repeated with
emphasis in verse 13 what he already said in verse 11: "Therefore
put on the full armor of God, so that when the day of evil comes,
you may be able to stand your ground, and after you have done
everything, to stand."

Another basic instruction of this seasoned spiritual warlord
before enumerating the armors is "stand firm." We would rather
consider this as part of the "armor" a soldier of Christ needs in

battle—the armor of courage—than mere instruction. This we shall do shortly.

Having given these very important instructions, Paul enumerates the following to constitute the armor of a believer: the belt of truth, the breastplate of righteousness, the readiness to preach the gospel, the shield of faith, the helmet of salvation, and the sword of the Spirit—the word of God. He then summarily adds: "And pray in the Spirit on all occasions with all kinds of prayers and requests. With this in mind, be alert and always keep on praying for all the Lord's people" (Eph. 6:18, NIV). This instruction seals the efficiency of all the armors he has mentioned. Without prayer "in the Spirit on all occasions" the armors may not be effective. This Pauline model will help us now understand more fully what a Christian, or an intercessor in particular, needs for spiritual warfare.

Standing Firm (Courage)

This principle is very important in warfare. It recalls the character of courage above. A soldier who is not firm on his ground, decisive and confident in his readiness to engage in combat, but feeble of heart instead, cannot hit the ground running or hit the target when he shoots. He is more prone to abandoning the war when it gets tough, or, even worse, becoming a deserter. An intercessor must therefore take his ground and stand firm courageously. He must be smart, vigilant, and poised for action. The importance of this instruction is underscored by the frequency with which Paul uses it in his epistles: "Be watchful, stand firm in your faith, be courageous, be strong" (1 Cor. 16:13); "Stand firm in the Lord" (Phil. 4:1, NIV); "Therefore let anyone who thinks that he stands take heed lest he fall" (1 Cor. 10:12). "Stand fast" bespeaks of being firm and focused, being on the alert, and avoiding any form of distraction in the battlefield. For it is only with this disposition that the weapons of war—defensive and offensive—can be effectively put into use.

It must always be born in mind that an intercessor is a soldier in the Lord's army. His field of battle cuts across the physical and the spiritual, even without his being conscious of this. He encounters and wrestles with men and spirits. As a spiritual warlord, an intercessor engages in diverse spiritual battles as and when required by his mission. For this reason, he is exposed to the danger of attacks by the enemy forces. His family and all that is dear to him are equally exposed to danger because when a chicken is caught, the mother hen would become an easy prey. This situation might put fears in an intercessor and make his heart faint. But no soldier who goes to war with fear, returns alive. A successful intercessor must therefore be a courageous soldier to be able to confront the enemy forces and contain the backlash that may be provoked by his mission.

Courage is one of the four cardinal virtues.[12] It is defined by *The Advanced Learner's Dictionary* as the ability to do something dangerous, or to face pain or opposition, without showing fear. It is related to the word *bravery*. It is the choice and willingness to confront difficult tasks, agony, danger, pain, or uncertainty without being intimidated by the threats of their rumblings. The *Catechism of the Catholic Church* uses the word *fortitude* for *courage* and defines it as "the moral virtue that ensures firmness in dif-

---

[12] "Four virtues play a pivotal role and accordingly are called 'cardinal'; all the others are grouped around them. They are: prudence, justice, fortitude, and temperance." *Catechism of the Catholic Church* (CCC), no. 1805.

ficulties and constancy in the pursuit of the good. It strengthens the resolve to resist temptations and to overcome obstacles in the moral life. The virtue of fortitude enables one to conquer fear, even fear of death, and to face trials and persecutions. It disposes one even to renounce and sacrifice his life in defense of a just cause" (1808). This is a very basic virtue that an intercessor requires to engage in his challenging mission.

God Himself has always required this virtue of those He calls and engages in one mission or another. He has no need of cowards. Moses was engaged by God because only a courageous man would do what he did, which forced him to flee the land of Egypt. He opted to perform an act of justice, regardless of the consequences. When God chose Joshua to replace Moses, He did so because of the role Joshua played in the group of twelve Moses sent out to spy out the land of Jericho. Ten of these spies gave an evil report and discouraged the people of Israel. When they returned from their mission they reported: "The land, through which we have gone to spy it out, is a land that devours its inhabitants; and all the people that we saw in it are men of great stature. And there we saw the Nephilim (the sons of Anak, who come from the Nephilim); and we seemed to ourselves like grasshoppers, and so we seemed to them" (Num. 13:32–33). With this evil report they made the people rebel against the Lord and make an ill decision to return to Egypt. But Joshua and Caleb rose up and courageously presented a report that showed absolute courage and faith in the Lord of the armies: "The land, which we passed through to spy out, is an exceedingly good land. If the Lord delights in us, he will bring us into this land and give it to us, a land which flows with milk and honey. Only, do not rebel against the Lord; and do not fear the people of the land, for they are bread for us; their protection is removed from them, and the Lord is with us; do not fear them" (Num. 14:7–9).

Indeed, the sons of Anak, who came from Nephilim, whom the ten spies dreaded, were great giants and renowned in the art of war. The people of Israel had at this time not learned the art of war and could not ordinarily compare themselves to the size and renown of these sons of Anak. This is admittedly an intimidating situation. Only with courage and faith in the Lord, who led their army, could they go out to confront these giants.

Courage is, however, not bravado, a blind march against destruction; nor presumption, an unguarded trust in one's ability or support. Courage here is a reasonable belief in oneself intelligently to pursue a justified cause on the ground that God will necessarily grant support. That was what Joshua and Caleb manifested. Thus, when God chose Joshua to take over for Moses, He repeatedly instructed him: "Be strong and of good courage; be not frightened, neither be dismayed; for the Lord your God is with you wherever you go" (Josh. 1:9).

David was anointed king over Israel for this same reason. The Lord saw the spirit of courage in him and knew that He had found a man after His own heart, a man who would lead His people and give them security and peace. When David was telling Saul about himself, he said, "Your servant used to keep sheep for his father; and when there came a lion, or a bear, and took a lamb from the flock, I went after him and smote him and delivered it out of his mouth; and if he arose against me, I caught him by his beard, and smote him and killed him. Your servant has killed both lions and bears; and this uncircumcised Philistine shall be like one of them, seeing he has defied the armies of the living God" (1 Sam. 17:34–36). He was not afraid to confront these dangerous wild beasts and did not fail to defend his sheep against their attacks.

He could face these dangers just for the safety of the sheep. This is a true shepherd. It is this devotion and courage that the Lord requires in His servants. This is why He chose David even as a boy. David's fortitude was clearly manifested when he resolved to engage Goliath in battle. Let us consider the background of this encounter:

> And there came out from the camp of the Philistines a champion named Goliath, of Gath, whose height was six cubits and a span. He had a helmet of bronze on his head, and he was armed with a coat of mail, and the weight of the coat was five thousand shekels of bronze. And he had greaves of bronze upon his legs, and a javelin of bronze slung between his shoulders. And the shaft of his spear was like a weaver's beam, and his spear's head weighed six hundred shekels of iron; and his shield-bearer went before him. He stood and shouted to the ranks of Israel, "Why have you come out to draw up for battle? Am I not a Philistine, and are you not servants of Saul? Choose a man for yourselves and let him come down to me. If he is able to fight with me and kill me, then we will be your servants; but if I prevail against him and kill him, then you shall be our servants and serve us." And the Philistine said, "I defy the ranks of Israel this day; give me a man, that we may fight together." When Saul and all Israel heard these words of the Philistine, they were dismayed and greatly afraid. (1 Sam. 17:4–11)

Like the sons of Anak, Goliath was very intimidating. He taunted the Lord's army and despised His name. Saul and Israel's army lacked the courage to engage him in battle. They were so terrified that they were speaking in hushed voices. But the Lord needed only a ready battle-ax to defeat Goliath. He needed just a fearless man, a man filled with courage, to humble him. He unfortunately found none. Then David arose and delighted the heart of God. He had not reached military age but came to the battlefield only to bring his brothers provisions. But the same spirit of a shepherd that steered him to kill lions and bears for the safety of his father's sheep could not be quieted. He therefore asked angrily and irritated, "Who is this uncircumcised Philistine, that he should defy the armies of the living God?" (1 Sam. 17:26). He could not understand why nobody was courageous enough to confront Goliath. He was disappointed and could not let Goliath insult the Lord and His army. He thus declared to Saul, "Let no man's heart fail because of him; your servant will go and fight with this Philistine" (1 Sam. 17:32). That was what the Lord needed to destroy Goliath and the enemy army.

Without the spirit of courage, no one will truly be in the service of the Master. When the Lord was giving laws for warfare, He instructed the army officers to proclaim to the soldiers, "What man is there that is fearful and fainthearted? Let him go back to his house" (Deut. 20:8). He repeated this instruction when He was gathering an army to keep the Midianites from oppressing Israel. He told Gideon to tell the thirty thousand men that gathered for battle, "Whoever is fearful and trembling, let him return home" (Judg. 7:3). Twenty thousand left the camp following this instruction. Only strong and courageous men and women are fitted for the arduous task of intercession. Cowards should go home. The Lord has no need of them.

The scenario shown above explains the encounters that men of God made in physical combats. However, the same principles observed in these encounters also apply in spiritual affairs. Spiritual warfare is not entirely different from physical warfare. They operate basically on the same principles. This is part of the reason the Old Testament is very useful. Sometimes people do not understand why God would send people to war or command them to destroy people, as commonly happens in the Old Testament. To understand it, we must carefully study the relationship between God and His people of old, and how He used special men and women in battles to score victory over His enemies. Deciphering his strategies in these encounters helps us understand what is required in our interactions with God and also when we engage in spiritual warfare today.

One of the most fundamental of these principles is the virtue of courage.

An intercessor should be ready to bear trials that might arise as a result of his spiritual deeds or the tests the Master might be pleased to send for the purpose of training and making him a seasoned soldier. Persecutions may also arise for other reasons. The devil may instigate hate against an intercessor to make his life miserable and force him to lay down his arms. It is for this reason that the Master told the prophet Ezekiel: "And you, son of man, be not afraid of them, nor be afraid of their words, though briers and thorns are with you and you sit upon scorpions; be not afraid of their words, nor be dismayed at their looks" (Ezek. 2:6).

An intercessor must also be able to react adequately to the urgency of his ministry and intervene timely in dicey situations. Sometimes this call could come at midnight, sometimes when one wishes to relax with friends or family. Sometimes intervention demands fasting and doing penance. An intercessor must be prepared to take the necessary pains and make the sacrifices required by the ministry of intercession.

A priest recounted an encounter he had with an angel of the Lord. This messenger of God visited him in the middle of the night to convey a very urgent message. A very important man in town committed a terrible evil and despised God. In anger the Master passed judgment on him, as He did on Israel, and sent the angel of death to strike him. This event was to take place in the territory this priest was working as a pastor. The Master offered the priest the respect and honor He offered Abraham when He wanted to destroy Sodom and Gomorrah, and Moses when He decided to wipe Israel off the face of the earth. Thus, the angel came to him in the middle of the night, woke him up, and told him that they were on a mission, he and the angel of death, to strike someone whose identity he also revealed to him. But the angel of death stayed outside so that the priest would not die. He told the priest that the Master said that He would not strike the evil man without informing the priest first.

The priest, as an experienced intercessor, knew immediately that the Master needed somebody to stop Him from bringing this disaster to pass. He needed an intercessor to intervene. He reasoned that He would not have informed him if He did not expect somebody to stand in the gap between Him and the offender. It occurred to the priest equally that the person in question would be dead by the next morning, that is, in a few hours, if the anger of the Master was not sated immediately. Because the identity of the person was revealed to him, he also knew what confusion and distress the sudden death of the victim would cause many.

He therefore pleaded with the angel to go back to the Master and tell Him that He should not do such a thing because of the sorrowful Passion of His Son. The angel implied that this visit was only to inform the priest, and that they would go on to complete their assignment. But the priest resisted his argument and insisted that if the angel had brought him the Master's message, he ought to go back to deliver his own message to Him too. The angel eventually obliged him.

As soon as the angel left, the priest went to his chapel to offer a votive Mass of the Sacred Heart of Jesus to atone for the sins committed by the person in question. After the Mass, he continued interceding till early in the morning, when the angel returned and thanked him for saving what would have been a very disastrous situation.

This urgent demand for intercessory assignment in the middle of the night could be demanding, and an intercessor must be strong to make such necessary sacrifices.

The Belt of Truth

Truth as used by St. Paul here refers essentially to the state of being sincere and authentic, of being genuine in serving in the Lord's army. It refers to the Lord's all-important word that those who serve God must serve Him in spirit and in truth (John 4:23). By extension, the armor of truth also touches on the authenticity of the deposit of faith that we keep. A soldier of the Lord must not believe in false religion or doctrines. With false doctrines, he finds himself on a false battleline and might easily play into the hands of the enemy. The teachings that are handed down to us through the apostles mark the course of the ministry of intercession and generally the Christian life. The belt of truth ensures that a soldier of faith wears these teachings very carefully. It secures the rest of the military uniform of a soldier of Christ as the physical military belt does, making movement in action freer and the soldier more comfortable to engage in battle. It behooves an intercessor, therefore, critically to study the path he treads and be sure that his Christianity is neither founded on the two extremes of fundamentalism and liberalism nor tossed around by every wind of doctrine. He must be a balanced and well-grounded Christian.

The Breastplate of Righteousness

The soldier of Christ is next equipped with the breastplate of righteousness. Soldiers wore a breastplate in ancient times, especially in the Greco-Roman world. It was very strong and impenetrable to swords and spears, and it was worn around the chest and the abdomen to protect the body's most vital organs. It is like a bulletproof vest worn by police and soldiers today.

Now, to protect the vital spiritual organs, an intercessor needs righteousness to act as his breastplate. Without righteousness, an intercessor is very vulnerable. The evil one can wound or even destroy him at will because his vital areas are unprotected.

Righteousness is accordingly an essential characteristic of an intercessor. It not only affords him protection against evil scheming but also helps his prayers to be effective. This is because sin is a terrible thing before God. The eyes of the Lord are too holy to behold iniquity (cf. Hab. 1:13), and the sacrifice of the wicked is an abomination to the Lord, but the prayer of the upright is acceptable to Him (cf. Prov. 15:8). God feels insulted and mocked when a sinner stands before Him, presenting his petitions without first humbling himself before God and confessing his sins. If this is the case, an unrighteous intercessor cannot succeed in his mission.

"The prayer of the humble pierces the clouds, and it will not rest until it reaches its goal; it will not desist until the Most High responds and does justice for the righteous and executes judgment" (Sir. 35:21–22, NRSV). If righteousness can exalt a nation (cf. Prov. 14:34), it can also exalt the prayer of an intercessor. God is holy, and those who encounter Him must also be holy according to their natures. This is why He commanded, "You shall be holy to me; for I the Lord am holy, and have separated you from the peoples, that you should be mine" (Lev. 20:26). Nothing unclean, therefore, must present itself before Him. He accepts only those who are pleasing to Him. No one can be pleasing to Him who is unclean. The letter to the Hebrews notes that without holiness, no one can see God (Heb. 12:14).

None of the great intercessors of the past trifled with holiness. When Daniel was in Babylon during the Jewish exile, he was very careful not to defile himself with the pagan meals and culture (see Dan. 1). This was a strong reinforcement for his prayers for his people. It was because Elijah refused to be a party to the abominations of his time that he was able to pray down God's decision on the land. David was a man pleasing to the heart of God. However, when he slept with the wife of Uriah the Hittite and killed Uriah to cover his sin, the Master dealt with him very roughly. This situation can help us understand why our Lady, the mother of Jesus, is a remarkably great intercessor. She is full of grace and lacks nothing as far as the holiness due to humans is concerned. This is why her intercessions succeed with the speed of lightning. It is therefore expedient that an intercessor must work to be holy.

God demanded much holiness from His people in the past, and this defines the field of God's operations. While the people of Israel were still on their journey to the Promised Land, the Lord gave them this instruction:

> You shall have a place outside the camp and you shall go out to it; and you shall have a stick with your weapons;

and when you sit down outside, you shall dig a hole with it, and turn back and cover up your excrement. Because the Lord your God walks in the midst of your camp, to save you and to give up your enemies before you, therefore your camp must be holy, that He may not see anything indecent among you, and turn away from you (Deut. 23:12–14).

The people were warned against "anything indecent" so that God would deliver their enemies to them. It is presented here as a pre-condition for victory. As a matter of seriousness, the consequence of indecency would be disastrous because rescue might be impossible if they got entrapped by their enemies. God has never ceased to demand sanctity from those who encounter Him. When He wanted to meet with His people at Mount Sinai, He also instructed Moses: "Go to the people and consecrate them today and tomorrow, and let them wash their garments, and be ready by the third day; for on the third day the Lord will come down upon Mount Sinai in the sight of all the people" (Exod. 19:10–11). Wherever the Lord moves, there must be decency and sanctity. This standard has not changed.

Now, if this level of material cleanliness was required of the people of God in the Old Testament, how much more would spiritual decency be expected of the children of the new dispensation, and particularly of intercessors? This is why St. Paul seeks only people who can lift up "holy hands" in prayer (1 Tim. 2:8). If an intercessor is unable to observe this rule, he may not participate in the ministry of intercession unless he first repents of his sins and returns to the Lord like David.

Purity is power. It can be a great treasure for an intercessor. Anyone who remains undefiled poses a great challenge to the powers of the underworld. He has beauty, like that of Mary Immaculate, which dazzles the diabolical. The intercessions of such people have always been fiery. Virginity and chastity are powerful spiritual dispositions in the intercession ministry. Can anyone remember the women in the lives of Elijah, Elisha, Daniel, and Paul? Married intercessors like Moses, Joshua, and Samuel succeeded because they remained strictly chaste. Such a commitment is required of any intercessor who desires to succeed. However, this is only part of what it takes to be holy. To be an intercessor demands a holistic sanctity.

The Boots of Readiness to Proclaim the Gospel

Now, the soldier of Christ is required to put on his boots. To serve as boots, St. Paul provided him with "the readiness that comes from the gospel of peace." That means that he must be filled with zeal to spread the fragrance of Christ according to his state and gifts. The ministry of intercession is one of the major ways of doing this. Thus, an intercessor puts on his boots when he zealously commits himself to making many experience the divine touch through his ministry and Christian living. With these giant boots of the zeal for his Father's mission, the intercessor can tread upon "snakes and scorpions" without being hurt and can bring Christ to many lost and distressed souls.

The Shield of Faith

Thereafter, the soldier of the Lord receives the shield of faith, with which he is equipped to extinguish all the flaming arrows of the evil one. Shields were also used by ancient Greco-Roman soldiers during battles. They would hold it in front of themselves with the left hand while wielding the sword with the right hand. It was basically a weapon of defense, which protected them from the blows of their opponents. It is this imagery that Paul uses to describe the function of faith in the life of a militant Christian.

Now, against the background that an intercessor is not a pure spirit but a human being with flesh and blood, he is impeded from being fully conscious of most of his spiritual encounters and escapades. He is not fully aware of his successes as a militant Christian. He is denied a complete knowledge of the number of souls he has been able to help and the number of evil forces he has succeeded in disbanding. He knows only a small percentage, if he knows at all. He also does not know why answers to some of his prayers are delayed or why some of his prayers are not answered at all. Sometimes it appears as if God is on a long vacation, when the intercessor receives no sign that He is still actively present.

These conditions create confusion and despair for the intercessor: he may sometimes think that his efforts are not producing any fruits or hitting the desired targets and thus may tend to become frustrated. He may even be tempted to think that God does not regard his efforts. But this is exactly why an intercessor should not work by sight but by faith. He must operate with absolute faith and trust in the Master whom He serves.

Faith is therefore a very necessary part of the equipment of an intercessor. According to Catholic teaching, "By faith man completely submits his intellect and his will to God. With his whole being man gives his assent to God" (CCC 143). Faith believes God completely and trusts Him absolutely. God is the center of the ministry of an intercessor. He has a complete knowledge of reality and is absolutely disposed to make the best decisions for His creation, especially man, and the intercessor is only a small but important instrument with a very limited knowledge of reality and the operation of the laws of existence. He must therefore submit to the wisdom of the Master to make decisions irrespective of the wishes and submissions of the intercessor. Thus, before he sets out on his mission, an intercessor must surrender to the absolute authority and will of the Master with the readiness to maintain the same attitude at all times. He should submit like Mary, the Mother of Jesus, and profess with her, "Behold, I am the handmaid of the Lord; let it be to me according to your word" (Luke 1:38).

Faith equally believes in the ability of the Lord as almighty and all powerful. It acknowledges that He can do all things (cf. Job 42:2) and that with Him nothing is impossible (cf. Luke 1:37). This lets the intercessor realize in every circumstance that God is in absolute control. Even though it may appear as if He does not respond or answer, He remains completely in charge. With faith the intercessor understands that God's ways are not our ways and that He has an appointed time for each of His works. Faith makes the word of God in the book of Lamentations concrete: "The steadfast love of the Lord never ceases, His mercies never come to an end; they are new every morning; great is thy faithfulness" (Lam. 3:22–23). The intercessor should believe in God's faithfulness with his whole being and be totally convinced that He does not fail those who hope in Him. When an intercessor prays, he prays with this conviction that God is faithful and trusts that He will act accordingly. We can use the prophet Elijah to illustrate how an intercessor uses faith to make things happen.

When Elijah prayed for rain after the great Mount Carmel contest and the massacre of the prophets of Baal, he attended the divine council to demand rain for the repentant Israel. But before he did that, he made a prophetic and faith-based utterance and told Ahab: "Go up, eat and drink; for there is a sound of the rushing of rain" (1 Kings 18:41). So Ahab went off to eat and drink, but Elijah climbed up to the top of Mount Carmel, bent down to the ground, and put his face between his knees. What was he doing? A seasoned man of God was getting ready to transport himself to the divine council to obtain the promise of God to send down the rain at the word of the prophet (cf. 1 Kings 17:1). Sometimes God's promises need to be converted to reality through faith-based intercessions.

Now, as Elijah prayed, he sent his servant to go and observe if a raincloud was gathering. Six times he sent the servant, who came back six times unable to give him a positive answer. Elijah stood on the pillar of faith relentlessly and insisted that heaven produce rain. He refused to give up until the Master fulfilled His promise. He sent the servant for the seventh time. This time the servant came back and said: "Behold, a little cloud like a man's hand is rising out of the sea" (1 Kings 18:44). This servant must have been a miser and a pessimist, with a discouraging spirit. But Elijah refused to be denied his miracle. He raised the armor of faith against the evil darts of doubt and discouragement by sending the servant to Ahab: "Go up, say to Ahab, 'Prepare your chariot and go down, lest the rain stop you'" (1 Kings 18:44). Shortly after that, the sky was covered with dark clouds, the wind started to blow, and a heavy rain began to fall. A man of faith can get heaven to work and make things happen.

Situations, however, arise that may challenge the fundamental truth concerning the faithfulness of God or cast doubts on the power of faith. An intercessor must, nevertheless, note that "in all things God works for the good of those who love him" (Rom. 8:28, NIV). He must always believe and trust the power of God and His faithfulness. He must resist the temptation to give in to thoughts and attitudes that suggest God's inability to save or that He is perhaps unfaithful. Don Moen has a song that expresses this condition: "I have made you too small in my eyes. O Lord, forgive me! I have believed in a lie that you are unable to help me. But now, O Lord, I see my wrong." An intercessor should never make God small in his own sight by believing in the lie that God is unable to intervene in the distressed conditions he presents to Him simply because He appears to delay His intervention or has a different way to approach the issues. He must not become oblivious of the fact that God works according to divine plans and not according to human plans. It was this unfortunate attitude that almost cost Elijah his prize as a great prophet of the Master.

The Lord did mighty things with the awesome prophet Elijah. The climax of His prophetic escapades was the duel with the prophets of Baal on Mount Carmel. On this mountain, the Lord answered by fire and "consumed the burnt offering, and the wood, and the stones, and the dust, and licked up the water that was in the trench" (1 Kings 18:38). The hearts of the people were then turned back to God and they confessed, "The Lord, he is God; the Lord, he is God" (1 Kings 18:39). After Elijah had destroyed the prophets of Baal, he prayed down a heavy rain after three years of drought. When Jezebel heard of what Elijah did to her prophets, she sent a message to him and vowed: "So may the gods do to me and more also, if I do not make your life as the life of one of them by this time tomorrow" (1 Kings 19:2). When Elijah heard this, he lost his confidence and became feeble. A mighty warrior of the Lord became very afraid and started to run for his life.

Why did Elijah become afraid, and why was he running away? Did he believe that He who had shown himself mighty in many ways in his prophetic ministry was now unable to protect him from the wickedness of Jezebel? This could be interpreted as making God small in his sight. He lost his courage as a great prophet and intercessor. He could not raise the armor of faith against these intrigues of the enemy. That did not go down well with the Master. God therefore needed to confirm the courage and faith of Elijah before He could use him further or award him His full prize. That was the reason He asked him to come to the mountain to meet Him. On the mountain, the Lord posed a challenge test that would confirm Elijah either as a courageous, faith-based prophet of the living God or a coward and faithless minister of the Master. His prize would be determined by the outcome of this test.

Thus, on the mountain, instead of meeting the Lord as he expected, Elijah encountered a strong wind, which blew until it caused the mountain to crumble and large rocks to break. This was followed by an earthquake and then fire. Obviously, this was a nerve-racking experience. It could cause a faithless servant of God to think that God was not there after all, even though He called him up the mountain to meet with Him. In this case, he would be making God a liar. The situation was indeed capable of raising doubts concerning the faithfulness of the Master in the mind of such servants of God as Elijah. A cowardly believer would run down from the mountain and abandon the appointment with the Master immediately after the whirlwind, the first session of the divine test. Naturally, Elijah must have been tempted also to run away from this terrible confrontation. But he must have also resisted the urge to give in to the temptation and be tagged a coward and faithless prophet at the twilight of his ministry. He must have said to himself, "He is a faithful God. If He called me to this place, He must then be here, behind these intimidating phenomena." Note that Elijah did not know that the Master was testing his courage and faith in him, just like

Job. He, however, endured the ordeal of these manifestations and regained the Master's confidence. It was only then that the Master appeared and tenderly called him, "Elijah!"

An intercessor must know and strongly believe that the faithfulness of the Lord towers beyond the heavens and would never buckle, no matter the condition. When He does not answer prayers, He has commensurate reasons not to do so. The maxim of an intercessor should thus be: "When God answers your prayers, you have faith in His abilities. When God does not answer your prayers, He has faith in your abilities." Intercessors who lack this basic characteristic would hardly win a case in the divine council because they have loaded guns without a trigger.

The Helmet of Salvation

A soldier puts on his military helmet to protect his skull from bullets or cuts from swords or strikes from clubs. Paul provides *salvation* to serve as this spiritual helmet. This armor refers to the hope of salvation as a sustaining force, as a reason for being steadfast in the battle. *Benson's Commentary* puts it well: "The helmet was for the defense of the head, a part which it concerned them most carefully to defend, because one stroke there might easily have proved fatal. Thus, it concerns the Christian to defend his mind, courage, and fortitude against all temptations to dejection and despondency, by a lively hope of eternal life, felicity, and glory, built on the promises of God, which ensure that salvation comes to those disciples of Christ, whose faith continues to the end to work by love."[13]

---

[13] Benson's Commentary on Ephesians 6, Bible Hub, http://biblehub.com/commentaries/benson/ephesians/6.htm.

After enumerating the defensive weapons, Paul now mentions the only offensive weapon in his idea of equipping a spiritual soldier—"the sword of the Spirit, which is the word of God." Although the sword could be used as a defensive weapon, it is better fashioned for offensive actions. Without it a Greco-Roman soldier would have no hope of striking and routing his enemy. In the next chapter, we shall discuss its nature and strategic position in the mission of an intercessor.

There are, however, some other important features, or, in Pauline terminology, armors, that an intercessor or a military Christian requires that are not covered in the Pauline passage above. We shall discuss them below.

Self-Immolation

The character of self-immolation is closely related to the character of courage because it is inspired and sustained by it. An intercessor who has these two qualities will be great in the Lord's army.

Sacrifice is a very operative word in intercession. This is because intercession demands selfless and committed service to others. No intercessor talks much of the self. An intercessor does not allow the self to choke his need to intercede for others. A schoolboy was once asked what part of speech *my* and *mine* are. He answered that they were aggressive pronouns—aggressive pronouns indeed! If an intercessor is still tied to the self, he is aggressively selfish and impaired in the tasks of intercession.

Every intercessor is like a candle, which cannot give its light unless it burns itself down; or like salt, which cannot offer its taste unless it dissolves and loses itself. The ministry of intercession demands self-giving. It involves a lot of sacrifice that cannot be expected to be simple. This is why Jesus underlines in John 12:24 that a grain of wheat remains just a grain unless it falls to the ground and dies. Here the Master is revealing that only by death comes life. The grain of wheat is in a state of passivity and therefore unfruitful so long as it is preserved, as it were, in safety and security. It is when it is thrown into the cold ground, and buried there, as if in a tomb, that it can bear fruit.[14]

According to Tertullian, a second-century Christian theologian, the blood of the martyrs is the seed of the Church. Like the seed one sows, it springs from the earth again, and fructifies the more.[15] That was the way Jesus died to save us. It was equally the strict asceticism of St. Dominic that combated and radically destroyed the Albigensian heresy (which will be explained later) that almost eclipsed the Church in the thirteenth century. It is really by spending life that life is preserved.

When the evangelist Christmas Evans was spending his life preaching Christ, friends advised him to take it easy. But should we really take it easy when many souls are heading to hell; when people are dying because of hunger and political intrigues; when the Church is sinking? The retort of Evans, however, was: "It is better to burn out than to rust out."[16] It should be noted here that the evangelist did not mean that it was a good thing to burn out, but rather that it was better than rusting out. A minister of God should, however, avoid the two extremes without failing to reach

---

[14] W. Barclay, *The Daily Study Bible*, vol. 2 (Bangalore: Theological Pub., 1994), p. 123.

[15] *The Apology of Tertullian*, trans. W. M. Reeve (London: Griffith, Farran, 1889), chap. 50.

[16] Quoted in James D. Berkeley, "Burning Out, Rusting Out, or Holding Out?", *Christianity Today* (Winter 1983), http://www.christianitytoday.com/pastors/1983/winter/8311036.html.

his target. He should keep on burning till the appointed end of his mission, and while he burns on, other candles will be lit.

When Pope Paul VI was canonizing the twenty-four martyrs of Uganda, he commented that they laid a foundation for a new age. The suffering and martyrdom of Charles Lwanga and companions brought not death but rebirth, a new life for Africa. If we must save others through the ministry of intercession, we must die to so many things. We must die to sin. We must die to self, vanity, worldliness, carnality, and all ungodly pleasures. We need to have more quiet time, going for desert experiences (the fasting and self-denial that liberates the spirit to commune easily with God), bending the knee and raising holy hands for hours, sending importunate prayers to heaven. We must be ready to accept every kind of necessary inconvenience for the sake of needy souls, if we are to be relevant as intercessors.

In 1998, a gang of hoodlums held some part of Imo State in Nigeria for ransom. It was a period of total collapse of security in the land. These criminals engaged in organized noxious criminality that people from this part of the state would not forget in a hurry. They were many in number and operated in the night as a team. In writing, they would inform certain villages or streets of their planned visit. They moved with buses and carted away people's property. The most horrifying aspect of their mission was their maiming, raping, and killing of their victims. It was a time of great terror and distress. This condition forced women and children to pass their nights in churches and the men in bushes. The government could provide no security, and the weapons the criminals wielded were sophisticated.

This condition became a great burden for one particular priest. He was deeply troubled by the sufferings of the flock that he and his colleagues were commissioned by the Most High to care for. He consequently resolved to take a special and urgent action to help the people. Though his resolve would be very taxing, he believed that heaven would not refuse to intervene. Thus, he requested ten decades of the Rosary daily from all his parishioners. Thereafter, he selected people from the different pious associations in his parish for spiritual warfare. With about thirty people, who were willing and battle-ready, he began a nine-day consecutive prayer vigil (10 p.m. to 6 a.m.). Night after night they cried to heaven and beseeched the Master for intervention. It was a great sacrifice — nine sleepless nights of unbroken spiritual warfare. But this is what the ministry of intercession means. It requires sacrifice — self-immolation. Such sacrifices are never in vain.

A few days after this warfare began, security was beefed up in the zone by the federal government. By the fifth day of the novena prayer vigil, five members of the deadly gang were arrested. Before the nine days were over, the rest of the members were rounded up. This spiritual war brought this period of terror to an end, and peace was restored.

An intercessor must not be afraid of dying, because the Master promised that He would restore his life again. In fact, Jesus said it point-blank that it is through losing life that the same life would be preserved. When St. Ignatius of Antioch was about to receive his martyrdom, he wrote in his *Letter to the Romans:* "How good it is to be sinking down below the world's horizon towards God, to rise again later into the dawn of His presence."

Wisdom

Another crucial quality an intercessor requires is the gift of wisdom. The Lord does not generally commission people with minimal common sense for great missions. A short story will illustrate this.

A river fish and a monkey were good friends. The monkey would collect fruit from the trees around the river and give some to the fish when the fish visited the monkey at the bank of the river. The fish would go back to her home under the water with this fruit and have a nice time with her family and colleagues. One day, the fish kingdom invited the monkey for a feast in his honor. The monkey was elated but was worried that he could not swim. The fish, however, promised to carry him on her back during the journey. On the day of the feast, the monkey dressed for the occasion and climbed on the back of the fish. In the middle of the spacious blue river, the fish said to the monkey: "Good friend, I have something to tell you, but I do not know how to say it." The monkey replied, "Friends should be free with friends and hide no secrets from them." The fish then told him, "I thought I should tell you this as a friend before we get to the feast. It is about the real reason why you are invited in our kingdom. We are preparing some medicine to protect us from predators, and the juju man requires the heart of a monkey for the medicine to become effective. That is obviously a hard task for us to accomplish. Our friendship, however, made you an easy target. That is the true reason we are on this journey."

The monkey was terribly alarmed. But seeing that he was trapped, composed himself and concealed his alarm. He immediately put his head to work and quickly designed an escape. "Faithful and good friend," he said to the fish, "this is why you are endeared to me. You are a very sincere and trusted friend. But why didn't you give me this information in time for me to get prepared at home for the mission. Now, you have inconvenienced yourself and your community. I thought you have always known that we monkeys are not used to traveling with our hearts. So, I left my heart at home, on that giant iroko tree where I live. My going to the feast without my heart is as good as a fruitless effort, and I'm sure your kinsmen will not be less than mad at you."

The fish was taken aback. Crestfallen, she asked the monkey what they should do. The monkey told her, "It is your decision, not mine. If you want to go to the feast without my heart, I'm okay with that, and if you decide to take the pain to go back so that we can collect my heart, I'm also comfortable with the decision." The fish turned back ecstatically and in utter disbelief that the monkey would agree to offer his heart. When they came to the bank of the river, the monkey jumped into the tree and said to the fish, "May thunder scatter your empty head, fool! Who have you ever seen moving without his heart, idiot? Go back and let your kinsmen use your own heart for the juju."

An intercessor with the head of this fish has already failed before even getting started. Like the monkey, an intercessor must be quick in thought and action. His eyes must be open to see and his mind fast to analyze and understand. If the intercessor is to succeed, he must respond quickly to the injunction of the Master: "Behold, I send you out as sheep in the midst of wolves; so be wise as serpents and innocent as doves" (Matt. 10:16). When Bishop Gregory Ochiagha was evaluating the words of Jesus above, he wrote:

> The loving wisdom of our Blessed Lord has said it all. The choice of the four creatures cannot be better. Sheep ordinarily have nothing in common with wolves. They are animals. Yes. But one is domestic and the other wild. Before the two can go together, the wisdom and watchfulness

of the serpent and the innocence of the dove must be perfectly and properly harnessed and blended in the sheep.
The serpent does not close its eyes. It is constantly on the
watch. If one may say it this way, it knows that a cock-
roach can never be innocent in the gathering of fowls.
Its life is constantly threatened. It does not therefore go
to sleep with the intention that all is well. The dove on
the other hand, is harmless. It is swift. It is calculated.[17]

An intercessor must possess the characters of these two creatures
(the serpent and the dove) perfectly harmonized in his life. This
is the only way he can saunter about in a wolf-infested zone without being mauled. He must therefore be wise. If the wolf outwits
him, he will be cornered and devoured. He must know whom he
is dealing with. He must understand him to anticipate his moves.
Wisdom could therefore be defined as the ability to make sensible
decisions and give good advice because of one's experience and
knowledge.[18] It means having insight, the ability to discern inner
qualities and relationships: a wise attitude, belief, or course of
action. One could describe it simply as good sense. Wisdom is a
positive productive interplay between knowledge, insight, and
judgment. It is important that an intercessor has some basic and
necessary knowledge about life generally and spiritual matters in
particular, develops a sharp sense of understanding matters that
are not beyond him, and acquires an ability to analyze situations
and make good decisions. This virtue is necessary because even
the divine council (on which he is a member) is not a council
of the ignorant but that of those with at least simple common

---

[17] Gregory O. Ochiagha, *Friendship* (Snaps Press, 2003), p. 5.
[18] A. S. Hornby, *Advanced Learner's Dictionary*, ed. Sally Wehmeier
(Oxford: Oxford University Press, 2012).

sense. The devil, who is the archenemy of the intercessor, is also so intelligent, cunning, and full of wits that an unintelligent intercessor would be an easy prey for him.

In the book of Proverbs and other didactic books of the Bible, God castigates foolishness frequently but praises wisdom. He clearly shows His disdain for foolishness and His admiration for wisdom. It is only in acting wisely that we manifest our resemblance of God, and that is why God praises those who act wisely. This characteristic helps an intercessor proverbially to walk on spikes without getting hurt. Consider the following story and figure out for yourself the role of wisdom (common sense) in the mission of an intercessor or Christians generally. The story offers also the opportunity to understand the relationship between wisdom and charity.

A lady had been falsely accusing a man, who loved God with passion and whom many looked up to as a Christian model, of inordinate advances. Both of them belonged to a small town in a suburb and worshipped in the same Catholic parish. She had told all in the suburb who cared to listen many ugly but false things about this committed, exemplary Christian. She had also made strong efforts to convince their fellow parishioners that he was not as innocent as they believed. Many did not believe her, but some were confused. In reality, however, the enemy only wanted to destroy this man's reputation as a way of checkmating his spiritual onslaughts against him.

One late evening, this man was driving home from the city, which was very far from the suburb. The sky was very dark and pregnant with heavy rainfall. People were packing their wares hurriedly and closing their shops. Everyone was hurrying to be home before the clouds let loose. The man passed a few panicky people waiting at a bus stop. Among them was the lady who had continued in her efforts to destroy the man's image. She frantically called out to him for help, since she was travelling to the same town as the man.

How should this man react? Stop and pick her up out of Christian charity or ignore her out of wisdom and drive home? A wrong decision here might be the beginning of unwarranted trouble for this respected man and possibly his destruction. The sufferings that might ensue from a wrong decision here would not result from any sin of the man or from any divine action or manipulation by the devil but would result purely from human folly.

Many have gone down because of folly, and many more are still going down. Jesus wanted His followers to live according to the dictates of wisdom. Hence, he commanded them, as already mentioned above: "Be as wise as serpents and innocent as doves" (Matt. 10:16). He followed this injunction and applied the principle of wisdom when the Pharisees and the Herodians set a trap for Him with the question of paying tax: "Teacher," they said, "we know that you speak and teach rightly, and show no partiality, but truly teach the way of God. Is it lawful for us to give tribute to Caesar, or not?" (Luke 20:21–22).

Although their approach was honey-coated, Jesus was not deceived— and not necessarily because of His divine attributes but rather because He was being as wise as a serpent. He could read in between the lines and differentiate a decoy from a dessert and flattery from genuine praise. Meanwhile, the Herodians and the Pharisees did not like each other and did not usually agree. Both also did not like Jesus. For them suddenly to agree and approach Him with this level of subservience and compliment was suspicious. These signs were enough information for a smart mind to be on alert and suspect that they had something up their sleeves. This was the stance of Jesus.

In response, therefore, He said to them, "Show me a coin" (Luke 20:24). When they gave Him a denarius, He asked, "Whose likeness and inscription has it?" And they replied, "Caesar's." Only then did He give His answer: "Then render to Caesar the things that are Caesar's, and to God the things that are God's" (Luke 20:25). Note that Jesus was very careful in approaching this question from which the Pharisees and the Herodians expected a yes or a no. Either of these would have put Him in big trouble, which the devil had long sought, and it would have been a result of folly.

An intercessor needs this level of common sense to wade through the convoluted spiritual world of his mission. We must recall here that many events of this physical world have spiritual backgrounds. Things are not always what they seem. Only through wisdom can an intercessor distinguish real gold from gold-coated metals and separate mere appearance from reality. The devil may appear as an angel of light to deceive an intercessor. This can happen in many ways but often through the sensitive spiritual gifts of prophecy and vision. An intercessor may not directly have these gifts (they are not a prerequisite for the ministry of intercession) but could get involved with people who have them or claim to have them. He must be able to discern properly and react intelligently.

The gift of discernment, which is meant for authenticating spiritual information and manifestations, is not a spontaneous, unbidden gift (like the gift of tongues); rather, it is the gift of insight and common sense. It is a gift that arrives at its end more through a process of careful reasoning and unbiased analysis. This was what St. Paul meant when he instructed the Corinthian Christians: "Two or three prophets should speak, and the others should weigh carefully what is said" (1 Cor. 14:29). The emphasis here is on "weigh carefully." To "weigh carefully what is said" means to consider reasonably the prophecy and prove whether it fits into the principles of divine operations or agrees, at least, with right reason. In this way an intercessor will avoid pursuing shadows or being deceived and consequently diverted from his mission. An instance of the use of the gift of discernment could be taken from the following experience.

A woman was sent to a team of prayer ministers to discern her claim of having the gift of prophecy. She had already given many prophecies in her prayer group, which had often spoken ill of the leader of the group publicly. Some other members, who were touted as having the gift of prophecy, had also confirmed that her prophecies were authentic, while some others were skeptical. The situation naturally created a palpable tension in the group. For this reason, the chaplain of the group decided to send the woman to a seasoned intercessory team for discernment.

The members of the team took her to a private chapel for prayer. Not three minutes after they started praying, the woman began to gyrate, stagger from one end of the chapel to the other, and eventually fall down. Now on the floor, she rolled herself up and down and began to "prophesy." The "spirit" speaking through her introduced himself as the Lord Jesus Christ. Her prophecy was coming in a direct speech. For some obvious reasons, however, the team doubted the spirit that was speaking through her and disagreed with his identity as the Lord. It rebuked the spirit, but he insisted that he was the Lord speaking.

Meanwhile, the woman, who was about seven months pregnant, continued to roll around, and the experienced team feared for her baby and her health and decided to end the prayer session immediately, though it had also completed its job. After the woman had gathered herself together, the team gave her the result of its discernment.

The team informed the woman that it could not see any sign that indicated that she had the gift of prophecy. The woman was visibly disappointed. She tried to explain to the team the points it was arguing with the "Lord" during her "prophetic" manifestations, insinuating that it misunderstood the message. Meanwhile, the discerning team knew that if the Master would speak directly through any human person, it would be a complete possession of the person. This means that his human instrument would be completely unconscious (temporary suspension of mental, intellectual, affective, and volitional faculties)[19] and would therefore have no idea of what transpired during this period. This kind of prophecy is equally strenuous and takes a lot of energy from the human instrument used. The woman, however, proved, with her explanations, that she was fully conscious, even as the alleged Master was directly speaking through her.

Again, the Lord knows in His great wisdom that He would not put such a pregnant woman through this kind of ordeal. Thus, no spirit was manifesting in the woman, neither a good spirit nor an evil one. She was simply faking a spiritual gift of her desire. This was the reason for her visible disappointment when she did not get a positive answer from the team. This is what is called discernment — being able to piece information together and discover the truth. Spiritual discernment has more to do with knowledge of spiritual operations and common sense. A careful observation and an intelligent analysis of data could tell the direction the spirit moves.

Another instance could be taken from one of the "prophecies" given by one of the "mega pastors" in Nigeria shortly before the presidential election of the United States of America in 2016.

[19] Amorth, *An Exorcist*, p. 61.

According to this pastor, he saw a woman win the election by a slight margin. Eventually it turned out that, in reality, a man won the election by a wide margin. The simple would excuse him because of the many miracles he is alleged to be performing. The wise, however, will write him off without discussion as no messenger of God. The entire scenario was nonetheless its own message from God, which gave His people necessary information concerning the real identity of this "prophet."

To understand further the status of this "man of God's" message, one has to look at the content. Does it serve any purpose? What does God intend by sending such information? If the content does not serve any serious purpose, it would then be classified as frivolity, and God does not involve Himself with frivolities or have an itching tongue. He cannot therefore be flippant. A careful perusal in the said message will indicate only that the "man of God" was merely seeking self-glory. He surely had followed very closely the campaign of Donald Trump and Hillary Clinton and the media prognoses about the outcome of the election, which could have offered him the ground to make a possible prediction. It would therefore at best pass for mere prediction, if he had gotten it right, and not a prophecy. However, the Master used the opportunity to give the wise a true message concerning the true identity of the "prophet."

An intercessor needs the wisdom that is required to distinguish the principles of the operation of the Master from both that of the enemy and of human pride and desires. The Master speaks to His own often but not necessarily in the way we commonly expect or imagine. He offers a lot of information indirectly and symbolically through people, things, and events happening around us. The carriers of these messages do not very often know that they are conveying divine messages. The messages may come in a complete or incomplete form. The incomplete form may come in a disjointed sequence, which may not be completed in a single day. It may take weeks or even months, as the case may be. An intercessor needs intelligently and patiently to piece these together and decode the divine message therein. For this reason, an intercessor must be a keen observer, a good listener, and smart in understanding and then working out the spiritual equation that will lead him to the message of the Master.

For a greater productivity through the functioning of this process, it is important that an intercessor should improve his knowledge through reading. He should be a diligent student of the Bible. He must not read it like a fundamentalist or study it as mere literature. The Bible should be studied to understand the divine mysteries and messages lying beneath the inscribed words. Knowing and understanding the teachings of the Church is equally crucial to equipping an intercessor. An intercessor should make efforts to improve his knowledge of the Church, her over two thousand years' history, and her teachings and interpretations of Scripture. He does not need to go deep into these matters like a theologian but needs to acquire enough basic information for his ministry. This background will be of immense help when the challenges of his ministry begin to unfold.

Steadfastness

The intercessory ministry requires patient forbearance and doggedness. It is for this reason that it needs people who are rugged and tough. The productivity of an intercessor will be paltry if he lacks steadfastness. This is because at times he may meet conditions that can make one doubt the efficacy and reality of what one is doing, as pointed out above. Sometimes answers to prayers are delayed or even appear unattended to. Naturally, this can lead to despair. But an experienced intercessor cannot allow himself to be intimidated or frustrated by this kind of experience. He does not give up easily or even at all. The experience of the great intercessor Daniel illustrates this situation very clearly.

When Daniel began to intercede for his people, who were in exile in Babylon, he probably did not set out to pray for three weeks. He was, however, disposed to beseech heaven until heaven responded. Perhaps he did not reckon that it would take three weeks. Nevertheless, he refused to budge when he got no answers. He continued his fasting and refused to relent on his tenacious supplications. It is in moments like this that an intercessor should pray even more unrelentingly. This is when he should become more insistent in his demands, reminding the Father of His promises, mercies, and faithfulness. He must refuse an answer of no or of silence, unless it is clear that it is a case of the absolute will of God (a knowledge that is very rare). There should be some element of stubbornness in an intercessor, the type that Jacob exercised when he wrestled with the angel. Jacob made it clear to the angel of God that his leaving him would depend on his blessing him. His approach was stubborn and insistent, and in this way he got what he wanted. Daniel was equally insistent and stubborn until the dawn of the divine answer.

Note that the prayer of Daniel was answered the first day that he began to pray. God sent His angel to him to give him the answer to his prayers, but because the kingdom of God is full of violence (see Matt. 11:12), Daniel had to fight on to overthrow the spirit prince of the kingdom of Persia (Dan. 10:13), who was keeping the angel of God from coming to deliver the answer to his prayers. He was thus engaged in a spiritual warfare but did not know exactly the extent of the spiritual energies he was releasing at the time he was praying. He was not fully aware of the adventures of his spirit in the divine council.

An intercessor must take seriously, therefore, the word of another seasoned intercessor, St. Paul: "We are not contending against flesh and blood, but against principalities, against powers, against the world rulers of this present darkness, against the spiritual hosts of wickedness in the heavenly places" (Eph. 6:12). The spirit of the prince of the kingdom of Persia was one such force that St. Paul was referring to. This spirit is, most likely, a national demon in charge of the ancient kingdom of Persia, which was a great kingdom (a world power) at the time of Daniel. His resistance could perhaps be because he was enjoying the slavery and suffering of the people of God, Israel, in Babylon and would not want them to have any respite. For him then, the idea of sending a messenger of God to them in any form must be resisted.

Sometimes we fail to get answers to our prayers because we refuse to pray our way through. We don't devote enough spiritual energy to counter the opposing negative spiritual forces. There are, no doubt, so many negative forces interested in our prayers, waiting to swallow them even before they get to the Master or swallow the answers before they reach us, like the dragon in the book of Revelation, waiting to swallow the child as soon as he was delivered (Rev. 12:4). Unless we understand that it is only men of violence that can take heaven by storm (Matt. 11:12) and consequently fight to the finish, our prayers or the answers to our prayers are likely to be aborted.

After heaven had already granted Daniel an answer by sending an angel to him, he was able to move heaven further through insistent and stubborn supplications. He sent importunate demands and refused heaven any peace. That indicated to the divine council that he had not gotten the answer that was sent to him. His petitions were revisited, and Michael the archan-gel was then sent to clear the way for the angel that was being resisted by the spirit prince of Persia. It was this resistance that delayed for three weeks the answer already given to the prayer of Daniel, which made it seem as if God had been silent to the prayer of Daniel.

Now, if Daniel had not insisted the way he did, perhaps the spirit prince of the kingdom of Persia would have devoured that answered petition. And if Daniel had given up after some days or did not hold on till he got an answer, how would the angel have met him to deliver his message? Who knows the number of petitions and answered prayers that have been lost through cold and feeble intercessions? And when this happens, we rage against God instead of against our inability to pray insistently and wait patiently upon the Lord.

An intercessor should not, therefore, stop praying until he gets an answer. His importunate intercessions can turn things around. Such intercessions can move the hand that moves the universe. If this were not true, Jesus would not have told us "to pray and not lose heart" (Luke 18:1). The request of His Mother at the wedding in Cana in Galilee helps us to understand how faith and persevering supplication help to obtain answers for our petitions. She told her Son, "They have no wine" (John 2:3). This implied a request of a mother who knows her son's ability to do something and save the host family from embarrassment. Although Jesus retorted, "O woman, what have you to do with me? My hour has not yet come" (John 2:4), His Mother was not dissuaded from pressing forward her request by believing that her Son would not refuse it. "Stubbornly" she went ahead and told the servants, "Do whatever He tells you" (John 2:5). Owing to this insistence of Mary, the divine order of events for the ministry of Jesus was adjusted. For Jesus told the disciples: "Fill the jars with water" (John 2:7). Lack of insistence, lack of perseverance in prayer denies intercessors the results they are meant to get from their prayers.

Like Elijah, an intercessor should insist on his request until he receives the full rain. Some people stop interceding when they see just a small cloud gathering. But it is a mistake to stop, because they were praying for a full shower and not for a rain cloud or just drizzles of rain. For this reason, many get only half measures when they could have gotten full measures. We must thus wait for the full manifestation of God before we lay down our arms. Otto von Bismarck said, "When I have laid for deer, I don't shoot at the first doe that comes to sniff but wait until the whole herd has gathered round."[20]

Moses could also have gotten a half measure if he did not pray to the finish and also allow Joshua to fight to the finish when Israel engaged in war with Amalek (cf. Exod. 17:8–16). It is remarkable that whenever the hands of Moses were raised (symbolically imploring heaven for help), Israel would gain the upper hand, but when they were down, Amalek would begin to subdue Israel. Aaron and Ur had to keep Moses' hands steadily up by using stones to support them until Israel had a landslide victory over Amalek. This is to say that in our intercessions, we should not leave our post until full victory has been scored. The holy hands of intercession must remain upraised until the dawn of triumph.

Intercession must thus be urgent and importunate. An intercessor should not give up even when God seems to pay no

---

[20] Quoted in Robert Greene, *The 48 Laws of Power* (London: Profile Books, 2000), p. 64.

attention. Jesus taught His disciples to be stubborn and insistent when they pray and never to give up, because "everyone who asks receives, and he who seeks finds, and to him who knocks it will be opened" (Matt. 7:8). This means that intercessors must ask until they receive, seek until they find, and continue to knock until the door is opened to them. It does not matter how long it takes, they must continue to pester heaven.

Steadfastness, therefore, means trustingly, patiently, and prayerfully waiting for the Master, believing that He will surely come. This is a manifestation of faith in the faithfulness of God. Thus, the prophet Habakkuk said, "For still the vision awaits its time; it hastens to the end—it will not lie. If it seems slow, wait for it; it will surely come, it will not delay" (2:3). This is part of the reason the Lord justified Abraham by faith. Abraham believed in the fidelity of the Master. One of the occasions of this manifestation of faith was when God booked an appointment with him for a ritual covenant. God directed him to prepare the animals for the ritual. Abraham gathered all the animals that were required for the ritual and prepared them according to tradition. But then he had to wait for the Lord till the going down of the sun. Abraham patiently and steadfastly waited for the Master, knowing that He would certainly come. While he was waiting, the birds of prey came to devour the materials for the covenant. But because he was awake while waiting, he was able to drive them away. He did not relent until the Lord eventually came and entered into an everlasting covenant with him (Gen. 15). An intercessor needs such a spirit of steadfastness and perseverance to guard his petitions from being devoured by the spiritual birds of prey until the dawn of divine visitation. Patience is a virtue. The Lord makes all things beautiful in His time. Many have missed the Master's blessing because they could not wait.

Chapter 4

The Art of Spiritual Warfare

After acquiring the essential features required for his ministry, an intercessor must also fill his quiver with the basic arrows needed for his mission before he sets out for battle. He uses these arrows as occasions present themselves. It is important to note that in the Pauline model of preparing for spiritual warfare, which we discussed in the preceding chapter, all the armor mentioned is meant for defense, except the sword of the Holy Spirit, the word of God. But now that the soldier of Christ is ready for war, he needs offensive weapons that can also serve as defensive weapons. First among these weapons is the word of God, which Paul called the sword of the Holy Spirit.

The Word of God: The Sword of the Holy Spirit

Words have power. According to Yehuda Berg, "Words are singularly the most powerful force available to humanity. Words have energy and power with the ability to help, to heal, to hinder, to hurt, to harm, to humiliate, and to humble." Words are mighty instruments to construct but also great weapons to deconstruct. With words, mountains can be erected, and with words, they can be razed. With words, things can be called into existence, and with words, they can be recalled into nothingness. Thus, the book of Proverbs wisely says: "Death and life are in the power of the tongue" (Prov. 18:21). The power of words must not be underestimated. Words have as much power to build as they have to destroy.

St. James elucidated the negative power of words in his epistle: "So the tongue is a little member and boasts of great things. How great a forest is set ablaze by a small fire! And the tongue is a fire. The tongue is an unrighteous world among our members, staining the whole body, setting on fire the cycle of nature, and set on fire by hell" (James 3:5–6). It is for this reason that the Master directs us to understand that words must be responsibly used, because they are not empty sounds or dead letters. He who is the Word of God Himself knows the power that men and spirits can wield with their words and the effects they can produce with them, and therefore warns in the gospel of Matthew: "I tell you, on the day of judgment men will render account for every careless word they utter; for by your words you will be justified, and by your words you will be condemned" (12:36–37).

That even the words of men are very powerful indicates that the words of Him from whom the Eternal Word proceeded can be exceedingly mighty. This was evidenced by the act of God when the earth was formless and void and darkness covered the surface of the deep. He then called things into being, and they came to be. John the Evangelist expressed this awesome manifestation of the power of words in the first chapter of his Gospel: "In the beginning was the Word, and the Word was with God, and the Word was God. He was in the beginning with God; all things were made through Him, and without Him was not anything made that was made." (1:1–3). It was this same Word that God sent to Mary through the angel Gabriel. Mary received this word by pronouncing her own word: "Behold, I am the handmaid of the Lord; let it be to me according to your word" (Luke 1:38). As soon as this fiat was pronounced, the Word became flesh in the womb of the Virgin Mary.

By this same power of the word, God can call things back from being. The psalmist professed: "Thou turnest man back to the dust, and sayest, 'Turn back, O children of men!'" (Ps. 90:3). Jesus recalled from being many sicknesses in many people through the power of the word and controlled the force of nature, when necessary, by the same power.

It is for this reason of the awesome power residing in words that St. Paul describes the word of God as the sword of the Spirit. In warfare, swords could be used to attack and to defend oneself or comrades. However, one could have a perfect sword for one's purpose but lack the knowledge of using it to achieve the desired ends. Therefore, before a soldier can wield the sword to produce desired results, he must first spend time and effort to become acquainted with the art of using the sword. This means that he must believe in what the sword can accomplish and carefully learn how to put it to good use. An intercessor must, in the same way, understand primarily the power in the Word of the Master and secondarily the power in his own words. He must equally learn the art of using the Word and his own words, too, in order to hit the desired targets. We will use a few passages from Scripture to highlight first the force an intercessor can set in motion when he properly uses the word of God as a sword and later his own words.

Any word that goes out of the mouth of God is destined to achieve a purpose, and it must of consequence fulfill its destiny, no matter how much opposition it may encounter. Consequently, it is written in the book of the prophet Isaiah: "So shall my word be that goes forth from my mouth; it shall not return to me empty, but it shall accomplish that which I purpose, and prosper in the things for which I sent it" (55:11). This is possible because the word of the Master travels with "lightning and thunder." The psalmist puts it in a very interesting way: "The voice of the Lord is over the waters; the God of glory thunders. The voice of the Lord is powerful; the voice of the Lord is majestic. The voice of the Lord breaks the cedars. The voice of the Lord strikes with flashes of lightning. The voice of the Lord shakes the desert. The voice of the Lord twists the oaks and strips the forests bare" (Ps. 29:3–9 NIV).

In the same way, Hebrews 4:12 says, "For the word of God is living and active, sharper than any two-edged sword, piercing to the division of soul and spirit, of joints and marrow, and discerning the thoughts and intentions of the heart." This text expresses the dual function of the word of God. It cuts across the spiritual and the physical. When it is set in motion, it must arrive at its destination whether it is within the human physical world (bone and marrow) or in the depth of the spiritual domain (soul and spirit). The word of God has accordingly no barrier whatsoever. Nothing can stop it from achieving its purpose or getting to its destination. Thus, the Lord says, "I work and who can hinder it?" (Isa. 43:13). No force can frustrate the power in the word of God. The mission of Jesus on earth was evidenced by the rampaging power of His words. Just a few examples will suffice:

- "Taking her by the hand He said to her, 'Talitha cumi'; which means, 'Little girl, I say to you, arise.' And immediately the girl got up and walked" (Mark 5:41–42).

- "And He came and touched the bier, and the bearers stood still. And He said, 'Young man, I say to you, arise.' And the dead man sat up and began to speak. And He gave him to his mother" (Luke 7:14–15).

- "When He had said this, He cried with a loud voice, 'Lazarus, come out.' The dead man came out, his hands and feet bound with bandages, and his face wrapped with a cloth. Jesus said to them, 'Unbind him, and let him go'" (John 11:43–44).

Those who acknowledge the authority of words exploit it in their relation to the word of God. This is how it becomes a sword for an intercessor. An intercessor should take a lesson from the Roman centurion, who sent a message to Jesus to heal his servant.

The Roman Centurion and the Power in Words (Luke 7:1–10)

A Roman centurion had a servant who was at the point of death. He wished he could help the servant live. He was told of Jesus. He sent messengers immediately to some Jewish elders to go to Him on his behalf and plead that He might come and heal his servant. When these elders came to the Master, they pleaded earnestly with Him with the following argument: "He is worthy to have you do this for him, for he loves our nation, and he built us our synagogue." The elders tried to put up a convincing argument. They showed their belief in the Master, that He had the power to do what they were requesting of Him, and supported their request with the fact that the centurion was a good man. Jesus heard their plea and set out to visit the house of the centurion and heal his servant. But then a very surprising thing happened. The centurion sent messengers to stop Jesus from coming to his house.

What was his reason? His message read: "Lord, do not trouble yourself, for I am not worthy to have you come under my roof; therefore, I did not presume to come to you. But say the word, and let my servant be healed." What a humble man! His attitude shows already how he sees Jesus in relation to himself. He holds Him in high honor and respect. With this message, he expressed his deep reverence for the Master. Though he did not want Jesus to come under his roof, he, nevertheless, needed Him to heal his servant. Thus, he added in his message, "For I am a man set under authority, with soldiers under me: and I say to one, 'Go,' and he goes; and to another, 'Come,' and he comes; and to my slave, 'Do this,' and he does it."

This is an extraordinary insight and manifestation of faith in the power of words (not necessarily the word of God). This man understands very deeply what we can accomplish with words when we have the authority to use them. A man under authority has the power to use words according to his office and achieve his desired ends. The centurion knows this and equally knows that Jesus is a man under greater authority. He expresses the fact that it is clear to Him that the authority of Jesus is more sublime and expansive than his. A centurion has power over a limited number of soldiers, but Jesus has power over nature, over all creation, including sickness. It then follows from his perception that Jesus needed only to use His authority, give the necessary orders through His word, and the sickness of his servant, like the soldiers under him, would obey. Then his servant would be healed. His understanding deeply surprised the Master. He was highly impressed by this centurion's rare knowledge and insight and praised his faith.

An intercessor requires this level of conviction and faith in the power of the word, primarily in the word of God and secondarily in his own words. If he does not use the word of the Master with absolute faith and pronounce it with total conviction in its efficacy, the power in the Word will remain inactive. In the same way, he should believe that he is the weapon of war of the Lord and should make decrees in the name of the Lord as one under authority. Studying the ministry of the prophets and how the New Testament speaks of the use of words (divine and human) will give us insight into how an intercessor should wield the power in words to make things happen.

Decree a Word

Jesus said to the Jews: "Scripture cannot be set aside" (John 10:35 NIV). This means much for an intercessor and helps him to appreciate the validity and efficacy of every word written in the Bible or spoken by the Lord. Hence, the word spoken in the book of Job could also be made to become real: "You will also decree a thing, and it will be established for you; And light will shine on your ways" (22:28 NASB). This was the case in an event that took place in a parish in Nigeria in 1999.

A little boy swallowed a fishbone, and it got stuck in his throat. It was a very bad situation. The mother had to rush him to the rural hospital. The house doctor could not help them but informed them that it required surgery, which could be handled only by a specialist. The bureaucracy required for doing this was odious, the hospital was miles away, and ambulances for urgent cases do not, of course, exist in this part of the world. And the little boy was choking. The parents were confused and, reasonably, very upset. They decided to take the boy to their parish priest. They believed that his prayers could help save their son.

After hearing their story, the priest realized that it was a complex situation indeed. Though he was equally intimidated by the report of the doctor, he knew that God had the power to intervene in such difficult situations. Incidentally, he was at prayer with a group of intercessors. He took the boy to this praying team, and they began to implore the Lord for help. As they were praying, the Spirit referred the priest to Ezekiel 37, where dead bones were made to live again through the decrees made by the prophet Ezekiel in accordance with the directives of the Lord. The man of God understood immediately what he was required to do. He exercised his authority as a Christian, a priest, and an intercessor and addressed the bone in the name of the Lord the Most High. He ministered the word of God to the bone, just like Ezekiel, and commanded it to obey the uncompromising power of the Word and come out of the boy's throat. He then dismissed them in faith. The poor parents left, unsure about what to do next with their child. But shortly after they left, the power in the Word was made manifest. The bone came out of the little boy's throat.

The word of God is as faithful as God Himself and can never disappoint those who trust in it. For "God is not human, that He should lie, not a human being, that He should change His mind. Does He speak and then not act? Does He promise and not fulfill?" (Num. 23:19, NIV). An intercessor must use the word of God efficiently in his ministry as the sword of the Spirit that it really is.

The Prophetic Power of the Word

Nothing lifts a troubled soul up from its distress like the word of God. The further prophetic power of the word of God resides, therefore, in proclaiming it as a weapon of war. An intercessor can thus use it when necessary to sooth and to anoint an afflicted soul. The encounter of Jesus with the Samaritan woman in the Gospel of John (chapter 4) clearly explains how the word of God could slice like a sharp razor through souls burdened with sin.

The woman at Jacob's well was languishing in sin when Jesus met her. Jesus saw her and knew that she needed the healing balm of the Word for her sick soul. To help her out of this lethal ailment, He began a ministration of the Word, which He started very casually but purposefully. The conversation continued until the Word hit its target and the woman realized her need of salvation. It is against this background that Justin Martyr, a second-century Christian apologist, declared: "His strong word has prevailed on many to forsake the demons whom they used to serve, and by means of it to believe in the Almighty God."[21]

A minister of God or an intercessor may not achieve much without an adequate grasp of the word of God. God does not send without the staff of His word. When He sent Jeremiah, He equipped him with His word: "Then the Lord reached out His hand and touched my mouth and said to me, 'I have put my words in your mouth. See, today I appoint you over nations and kingdoms to uproot and tear down, to destroy and overthrow, to build and to plant'" (Jer. 1:9–10). When He was preparing Ezekiel, He had to give him His word to masticate: "'Son of man, eat what is before you, eat this scroll; then go and speak to the people of Israel.' So I opened my mouth, and he gave me the scroll to eat. Then he said to me, 'Son of man, eat this scroll I am giving you and fill your stomach with it.' Then I ate it; and it was in my mouth as sweet as honey" (Ezek. 3:1–3).

Now, this is how every minister of God, everyone involved in the ministry of drawing souls to heaven, should eat and get acquainted with the word of God. Scripture must be part and parcel of the arrows in his quiver. The message of his mission is contained in that scroll. If he does not eat it and "fill his stomach

---

[21] Justin Martyr, *Dialogue with Trypho*, no. 83.

with it," he will probably deliver his own message because he will lack a message to deliver. This is the reason homilies and sermons can be dry and insipid. They lack the touch of the word of God, which bears the essence of the message that saves. Homilies or sermons might turn the audience on and titillate their fancy but might not convert a soul or achieve any spiritual effect. They will at best be entertainment, for they are words preached from the wisdom of man. When a man of God is soaked with the word of his Master, he will deliver the fiery message of his Father. This is because, through his interactions with the word of God, he is inspired by the Spirit, who owns the word as a sword. This is the way sermons or homilies can pierce through the marrow of the soul and change lives and situations. Any sermon short of this can at best impress the intellect but will not enrich the soul.

When Jesus was commissioning His disciples, He asked them: "'When I sent you without purse, bag, or sandals, did you lack anything?' 'Nothing,' they answered. He said to them, 'But now if you have a purse, take it, and also a bag; and if you don't have a sword, sell your cloak and buy one'" (Luke 22:35–36, NIV). They showed him two swords and He said, "It is enough." What does this sword represent? Our text above calls it the sword of the Spirit. Jesus knows the great importance of the word. He made His disciples abundantly aware of this. It is more important than one's coat (that is, something for covering one's nakedness and protecting the body from cold). In the thoughts of the Master, it is more important than even covering one's nakedness. The disciples understood this and made profuse use of it.

During the Hellenistic food crisis, the apostles said, "It would not be right for us to neglect the ministry of the word of God in order to wait on tables" (Acts 6:2, NIV). The position of the word in the mission of a believer is pivotal. In spiritual warfare, its use is as invaluable as it is inevitable. A believer, an interces-sor, a man of God, must possess a Bible, consume the contents, and be acquainted with it, if he is to be worth the name.

Praying with the Word

An intercessor prays with the word of God. His prayers will be swifter when they are supported by the testimony of the word. If we observe the prayers of great men and women of God in the Bible, we will see that they rarely prayed without reference to the word of God. This reference gave their prayers character, a trademark, and in this way made them glide more swiftly to the divine council.

During the exile of the Jews, Daniel prayed thus: "Now, Lord our God, who brought your people out of Egypt with a mighty hand and who made for yourself a name that endures to this day, we have sinned; we have done wrong" (Dan. 9:15, NIV). Daniel was invoking what was recorded in the Scriptures about the might of God and the favors He showed their ancestors. He used this appeal to the books of the law as a background for his supplication. This gave his petition more weight, as we have mentioned earlier while discussing the intercession of Moses.

When Haman instigated a conspiracy to annihilate the Jews, Queen Esther fired an intervening prayer:

> O! My God, thou only art our King: help me, who am alone and have no helper but thee, for my danger is in my hand. Ever since I was born I have heard in the tribe of my family that thou O Lord didst take Israel out of all the nations and our fathers from among all the ancestors, for an everlasting inheritance and that thou didst do for them

all that thou didst promise. And now we have sinned before thee.... O! Lord do not surrender your scepter to what has no being. (Esther 14:4–11)

A reminiscence of the deeds and words of God can help drive home one's petitions. It makes a request more appealing and gives the petition authority. Esther exploited this as Daniel did, and it yielded a harvest of victory.

During their period of persecution the apostles also offered this powerful prayer:

Sovereign Lord, you made the heavens and the earth and the sea, and everything in them. You spoke by the Holy Spirit through the mouth of your servant, our father David: "Why do the nations rage and the peoples plot in vain? The kings of the earth rise up, and the rulers, and together against the Lord and against His anointed one" (cf. Ps. 2:1–2). Indeed, Herod and Pontius Pilate met together with the Gentiles and the people of Israel in this city to conspire against your holy servant Jesus, whom you anointed. They did what your power and will had decided beforehand should happen. Now, Lord, consider their threats and enable your servants to speak your word with great boldness. Stretch out your hand to heal and perform signs and wonders through the name of your holy servant Jesus (Acts 4:24–30, NIV).

The effect of this prayer could only be imagined from what happened after: the house in which they were staying shook and they were filled with the Holy Spirit. This powerful prayer was succeeded by great manifestations in their witnessing. Praying with the word of God gives the petitions of an intercessor authority.

That is why it is important that an intercessor should know the Bible adequately.

The Holy Eucharist

Another arrow that should be found in the quiver of an intercessor is the Eucharist. Jesus said, "Very truly I tell you, unless you eat the flesh of the Son of Man and drink His blood, you have no life in you. Whoever eats my flesh and drinks my blood has eternal life, and I will raise them up at the last day. For my flesh is real food and my blood is real drink. Whoever eats my flesh and drinks my blood remains in me, and I in them" (John 6:53–56, NIV). Shortly before He was taken away to be slaughtered as the sacrificial Lamb, He officially instituted a sacred event, which made it clear how the words above should be understood and actualized.

Thus, while He was sitting at supper with His apostles, Jesus took bread, broke it, and gave it to them, saying: "Take and eat; this is my body" (Matt. 26:26). In the same way He took the cup after supper and said: "Drink from it all of you. This is my blood of the covenant which is poured out for many for the forgiveness of sins" (Matt. 26:27–28). Thereafter, He went to Calvary to be sacrificed and for His Body and Blood to be concretely given up for the life of many.

The three synoptic writers and St. Paul recorded this account meticulously. Each recorded it in direct speech. Jesus insisted in all these records that what He was giving were His very Body and very Blood, just as He told the Jews in the Gospel of John cited above. At no time did He say: "This is a symbol of my body, and this is a symbol of my blood." What He gave His followers was rather that Body which He gave up for all men and all women, for their salvation. It is the Body broken to make us whole again. He gave us that Blood poured out for many, those that are to be saved, so that sins may be forgiven. To make sure we have this wonderful spiritual food always, He added, "Do this in remembrance of me" (Luke 22:19; cf. 1 Cor. 11:25). In this way, He gave His apostles and their successors the authority to consecrate bread and wine so that they would become His Body and Blood.

This promise can then be actualized only through the breaking of bread, the sacrifice of the Mass. At every Mass, therefore, Calvary is transplanted to the altar and the events that took place more than two thousand years ago are made actual once again. From this wonderful sacrament an intercessor can draw more strength than he can imagine.

This does not need any rationalization to understand. It does not require any philosophical inquiry. This biblical reality asks only for a simple faith. No matter how metaphorically one tries to interpret the words of Jesus here, as some have preferred to do, the simple and direct statement of our Lord in these biblical passages remains absolutely and nonfiguratively real. It is a statement of fact to be believed without any semantics or theological quibbles. Christians have believed and practiced this tradition right from the Last Supper, when it was instituted. They called it the "breaking of the bread" (Luke 24:35; Acts 2:42). For every believer who accepts this as the word from the holy lips of the Master, it becomes a powerful source of grace.

It is understandable, however, that one may hesitate to accept this teaching. How is it that an ordinary man called a priest can say some mystic prayers ordained by the Church over some bread and wine and they become the Body and Blood of the crucified Lord, Jesus Christ? This might be your pattern of thought. But listen to this experience.

During a deliverance session a priest encountered a demon that had possessed a young girl for some years. The demon was tough and obstinate. He so resisted forfeiting the temple he had taken over that the priest was tempted to despair. The praying team was already becoming demoralized and discouraged. But then a thought came to him: "Take him to the Eucharistic Jesus." In the chapel, the Eucharistic Lord was brought out to stand as a great King reigning in the effulgence of glory and splendor from the monstrance on the altar. The tide of events changed immediately. The demon shouted at the top of his voice and with great fright, "Who is this! Who is this person?" For him, the Eucharist is "who" and "person," but for a nonspiritual eye it is "what" and "thing." We might be seeing a white round substance, but the demons see a person, the Master in His glory. The demon saw the glory of God filling His temple and was dazed. He closed his eyes. He was now stuttering, "Let me go. I don't want to see Him. Who brought me to His house? We don't like each other. Take me out of this place!"

"My God! What is he talking about?" the young priest thought to himself. "Is he addressing the consecrated bread on the altar? But it was just this morning that I consecrated it at Mass. How could it be this powerful?" He reasoned myopically like the priest Zechariah, who ministered in the Holy of Holies but could still not believe the words of the archangel Gabriel.

Since the priest entered the chapel with the prayer ministers, nobody had said any other prayer outside the chants: "O Sacrament Most Holy, O Sacrament Divine, all praises and all thanksgiving be every moment thine." At that very moment it dawned on the priest that the consecrated bread was more than what it appeared to be. It is our Lord. It became the Lord in flesh and blood after consecration. Though He is in the form of bread and wine, He remains God and identifies himself as "the Lord, who heals you" (Exod. 15:26, NIV); the wounded Healer and the bleeding Messiah (Isa. 53:5); "the Lion of the tribe of Judah" (Rev. 5:5). After the Consecration, the Church calls this bread *Sanctissimum*, which means the "Most Holy," and only God can take this title.

The "Man of war" (Exod. 15:3, KJV) was going to war, and the kingdom of this demon, who had been tormenting this young girl for some years, was badly threatened. When he saw that he had been cornered, he decided to engage the Master in a fight. His plan was to push Him down from the altar. At first, the praying team tried to protect the Lord from being pushed down, but after some thought, the priest felt that He should be allowed to fight for Himself and asked the prayer ministers to let the demon do what he wished. The demon then rushed with a terrific speed and force toward the altar. But just an inch away from the altar, he stopped with an automatic halt, as if controlled electronically. He tried again and repeated the first experience. He drew back the third time, mustered all his strength and courage and tried again. This time he succeeded having a brush with the altar cloth. It was then that hell was let loose on him. The demon was rattled. He was thrown up high and dashed with a heavy thud on the hard floor and set into a bout of rolling, wriggling, and shouting until he begged to leave.

The Eucharistic Jesus is a mighty force against the devil. The devil sees in the *Sanctissimum* the crucified Jesus as He really is. A human cannot see this except with the eyes of faith. This is why it is called a sacrament — the bread is a sign of the invisible reality behind it. The Church duly acknowledges the power in the consecrated bread and has given it a home in tabernacles found in millions of churches and chapels throughout the world.

She did this in order to make the Lord sacramentally present in these places so that believers could go there to adore Him and also to present their troubles to Him and be healed.

Because Jesus Himself is at every Holy Mass, wonderful miracles are experienced daily by very many people throughout the world each time the Mass is celebrated. At this sacred time, the Lord is fully present, the events of Calvary are once again enacted, sinners are made clean, the despondent strengthened, the sick receive healing, and prayers answered. Fr. Emiliano Tardif, who died in June 1999, had a spectacular gift of healing. Many people throughout the world received healing through his grace-filled ministry. Worthy of note in his ministry is that it was very closely connected with the Holy Mass. Within the Mass or just after it, he would receive a word of knowledge about those who were to be healed or being healed. When he began to pray, the glory of the Lamb that was to be slain or was just slain at the Mass would begin his ministry of healing. According to Fr. Tardif's personal testimony of what happened in Nagua (Dominican Republic): "We celebrated the holy Mass and the Lord began once again to heal the sick.... He healed on that Sunday not only two or three sick people but a tremendous crowd."[22]

The effect of the Mass continues after the Mass through the consecrated Bread preserved in the tabernacle and worshipped as the Lamb of God. Catholics believe in the Real Presence of the Lord in the Eucharist and therefore offer Him a practical home among them. They go there to encounter Him for various reasons. An intercessor, who makes adequate use of this arrow in her quiver, told the story of a woman who bore a pregnancy for

---

[22] Emiliano Tardif and Jose H. Prado Flores, *Jesus Lebt* (Münsterschwarzach: Vier-Türme-Verlag, 1988), p. 20.

three calendar years. According to the story of this woman, her ordeal was a result of witchcraft. An evil agent placed a diabolical curse of perpetual pregnancy on her. She went to all forms of hospitals, met different gynecologists, and visited many prayer houses but could not be helped. She was eventually introduced to the Eucharistic Jesus. In a chapel of perpetual adoration, she was asked to talk to the Eucharistic Lord, who was exposed in a monstrance, about her problems.

Incidentally, this woman was a Protestant and did not understand the Catholic theology of the Eucharist. The intercessor gave her a crash catechism on the theology of the Eucharist. She was taught that what she was seeing in the monstrance was not actually a round white substance, but the Lamb of God slain on Calvary's tree; that He was still bleeding to save those who call upon His name, and that if she believed, she would be healed. She then shouted, "Lord, I believe. Lord, I believe." She was left alone with the Lord for some time to pour out her pains and sorrows to Him who alone could deliver her. The intercessor, who brought her for this encounter, eventually called for a priest who came into the chapel, spoke some authoritative words over her, and sent her home, as Eli did Hannah (cf. 1 Sam. 1:17). Three days later, she gave birth to a healthy baby girl.

With such manifestations, believers continue to realize that "the reason the Son of God appeared was to destroy the devil's work" (1 John 3:8, NIV). What prevents an intercessor then from invoking this power for positive wonderful results? Many miracles are being recorded from encounters with the Eucharistic Lord daily in Holy Masses, Eucharistic adorations, and other Eucharistic activities throughout the world.

One such testimony is that experienced by a young girl who was under satanic oppression. She was once attacked in a dream by some unknown men who almost throttled her to death. When she got up, her throat was swollen and full of pain. She could hardly speak or swallow anything. She was asked if she could receive Holy Communion. She affirmed her readiness in accordance with the Catholic tradition. She was taken to the chapel and a priest ministered Holy Communion to her as he would the sick. This daughter of Abraham came back to this priest after about two hours to praise the glory of this wonderful sacrament. She was completely healed. Is this not the fulfillment of the prophecy of Isaiah: "With His stripes we are healed" (Isa. 53:5)?

Fr. Tardif also gave the testimony of a man who was brought forward on a stretcher during a Mass, as he was testifying to his own personal healing. This man's backbone was broken, and he became, as a result, lame for five and a half years. They prayed for him and pleaded with the Lord specifically to heal him through the power of His holy wounds. According to Fr. Tardif, the sick man began to sweat heavily and to shiver. The priest knew exactly what that meant and spoke authoritatively: "The Lord is about to heal; stand up in the name of Jesus." He gave him his hand and encouraged him to get up and walk. The man did but slowly. The man of God spoke again: "In the name of Jesus, go further, the Lord is present to heal you."[23] And the Lord made him whole once again. Such is the power of the Lord in the Eucharist.

An intercessor, who identifies with Jesus in the Eucharist, can handle difficult cases. He does not just end with the invocation of this treasure. He must, as often as possible, be part of the Sacrifice of the Mass through which this power flows. He must also dispose himself to partake of the wondrous meal served at each Mass.

[23] Tardif, *Jesus Lebt*, p. 18.

This meal gives him protection and strengthens him along the path of righteousness. He needs it to stand in the spiritual battle. Elijah had a foretaste of this sacrament when God was preparing him for that great journey to the mountain (see 1 Kings 19:5–7). God sent an angel who brought him some bread and water to strengthen him for the strenuous journey ahead. The angel said to him, "Arise and eat, else the journey will be too great for you" (1 Kings 19:7). This is how God, through the sacred bread from heaven, strengthens His soldiers on the battlefield.

The people of Israel ate the Passover in Egypt and smeared the blood of the lamb on their doorposts in order to be protected from the angel of death. These Old Testament experiences prefigured the reality we experience today in the Eucharist. It was for this reason that Jesus told the Jews: "Truly, truly, I say to you, it was not Moses who gave you the bread from heaven; my Father gives you the true bread from heaven. For the bread of God is that which comes down from heaven and gives life to the world" (John 6:32–33).

Alessandro, an Italian living in Rome, gives testimony that confirms the power in the Eucharist. According to him, the devil tormented him physically for five years. He had the sensation that needles were stuck in every part of his body, especially in his vital organs. He felt bitten, stabbed, and other similar sensations. He visited many exorcists in Rome and joined various charismatic prayer meetings with the hope for deliverance. But none brought him healing. He finally found a path to complete healing, however, in daily Mass and in fasting. His words: "In my experience, this is the most powerful way to deliverance, besides confession of sins and Communion."[24]

---

[24] Amorth, *An Exorcist*, p. 55.

To discover the Eucharistic Jesus is to discover a priceless treasure, and to work with Him is the root of power and success. Intercessors, who wish to be equipped and clothed with power and the strength to be firm and productive, gather often before Him and worship Him with spirit-filled adoration.

The Power of Praise

Praise is another powerful arrow that must be in the quiver of an intercessor. The book of praise, the book of Psalms, notes that God dwells in the praises of His people: "But you are holy, O you that inhabit the praises of Israel" (Ps. 22:3, KJV). If there is anything that delights the heart of God, if anything thrills Him, it is the praise and thanksgiving, worship and adoration offered by His creatures, especially those made in His image and likeness. He highly relishes the praise of His people. If we watch closely how His abode in heaven is structured, we would discover that it is organized in such a way that there will be unbroken worship and praise of His glory.

The vision of Isaiah saw the Lord, high and exalted, seated on a throne and seraphs at worship singing: "Holy, holy, holy is the Lord of hosts; the whole earth is full of His glory" (Isa. 6:3). Daniel saw thousands upon thousands of angels ministering to God. Ten thousand times ten thousand were surrounding His throne (cf. Dan. 7:10). The mission of these angels is to attend to the glory of God. It is their function to minister praise and worship to Him day after day unceasingly. The vision of John is even more eloquent:

Round the throne were twenty-four thrones, and seated on the thrones were twenty-four elders, clad in white garments, with golden crowns upon their heads. From the throne issue flashes of lightning, and voices and peals of thunder, and before the throne burn seven torches of fire, which are the seven spirits of God; and before the throne there is as it were a sea of glass, like crystal. And round the throne, on each side of the throne, are four living creatures, full of eyes in front and behind: And the four living creatures, each of them with six wings, are full of eyes all round and within, and day and night they never cease to sing, "Holy, holy, holy, is the Lord God Almighty, who was and is and is to come!" (Rev. 4:4–6, 8)

Note that John saw the same vision that Isaiah saw and heard the same pattern of worship that Isaiah heard. When Jesus was born, these angels of praise followed their now incarnate Master to the earth, worshipping Him still. According to Luke, "And suddenly there was with the angel a multitude of the heavenly host praising God and saying, 'Glory to God in the highest, and on earth peace among men with whom He is pleased!'" (Luke 2:13–14).

This shows that God has always been dwelling in the praises of His creatures. For all eternity God is praised, from everlasting to everlasting. John's visions in the book of Revelation underscore the reality that the panorama of heaven is a perpetual praise-worship. We quote a part of his vision here to emphasize this reality:

And when He had taken the scroll, the four living creatures and the twenty-four elders fell down before the Lamb, each holding a harp, and with golden bowls full of incense, which are the prayers of the saints; and they sang a new song, saying, "Worthy art thou to take the scroll and to open its seals, for thou wast slain and by thy blood didst ransom men for God from every tribe and tongue and people and nation, and hast made them a kingdom and priests to our God, and they shall reign on earth." Then I looked, and I heard around the throne and the living creatures and the elders the voice of many angels, numbering myriads of myriads and thousands of thousands, saying with a loud voice, "Worthy is the Lamb who was slain, to receive power and wealth and wisdom and might and honor and glory and blessing!" And I heard every creature in heaven and on earth and under the earth and in the sea, and all therein, saying, "To Him who sits upon the throne and to the Lamb be blessing and honor and glory and might for ever and ever!" And the four living creatures said, "Amen!" and the elders fell down and worshiped. (Rev. 5:8–14)

What do we imagine God doing while the whole of this magnificent activity is going on? Surely, sipping and relishing this organized praise and worship of His Person. He really does enjoy praise-worship. In His wisdom, He planned it to be so, for His pleasure (see Rev. 4:11). The Catholic tradition holds that there are three hierarchies of angels, each of which contains three orders, or choirs: Angels, Archangels, and Virtues; Powers, Principalities, and Dominions; Thrones, Cherubim, and Seraphim. St. Gregory the Great teaches:

We know on the authority of Scripture that there are nine orders of angels, viz., Angels, Archangels, Virtues, Powers, Principalities, Dominations, Throne, Cherubim and Seraphim. That there are Angels and Archangels nearly every page of the Bible tells us, and the books of the Prophets talk of Cherubim and Seraphim. St. Paul, too, writing to the Ephesians enumerates four orders when he says: "above all Principality, and Power, and Virtue, and Domination"; and again, writing to the Colossians he says: "whether Thrones, or Dominations, or Principalities, or Powers." If we now join these two lists together we have five Orders, and adding Angels and Archangels, Cherubim and Seraphim, we find nine Orders of Angels.[25]

St. Thomas Aquinas, the Angelic Doctor, essentially teaches the same doctrine as St. Gregory the Great.[26] Each of the angelic choirs has a membership of a multitude of angels equipped with assorted kinds of musical instruments to celebrate the glory of the One on the Throne and of His Lamb. To this number is added an uncountable number of saints — the spirits of the just made perfect (see Heb. 12:23) — all meant for the praise and worship of the Triune God. This is the reason for their existence. Thus, Isaiah declares that we are created for His glory (see 43:7).

It is important that intercessors should learn the power of praise. A group of prayer ministers may gather for hours praising God and soaking the air with divine waves. It is sometimes preferable not to "bother" God with long chains of petitions. Believers should also learn to offer Him a sacrifice of praise, which He cherishes most. David, the king of praise, knows and teaches us that the power of God is at its best in praise. The psalms, generally called the psalms of David, are replete with praise, worship, and thanksgiving. David, who composed most of the psalms, knew where to touch God so He would respond. Was

---

[25] Gregory the Great, *Homiliae xxxiv in Evangelia*.
[26] Thomas Aquinas, *Summa Theologiae* I, q. 108.

his life not full of success? Was he not a conqueror? His slogan was: "The praise of God on the lips and a two-edged sword in the hand" (see Ps. 149:6).

The Father cherishes it when His awesome deeds are recounted and His person is addressed accordingly. He likes being identified with His great works and addressed with names that portray His might and wondrous manifestations. When He is qualified with the great attributes due His name, He displays them further in His new works because He is always doing a new thing (see Isa. 43:19).

Praise was the secret of the men of old. They knew how to address the Master and move Him to do mighty things. An intercessor could use those names or attributes that were revealed to these noble men and women to worship God in the beauty of His holiness. For instance, He revealed himself to Moses as "I AM WHO AM" (see Exod. 3:14); Moses described Him as the "God of gods and Lord of lords, the great God, mighty and awesome" (Deut. 10:17, NIV); Samuel worshipped Him as "Ebenezer—Stone of help" (1 Sam. 7:12, NIV); David adored Him as "the Lord of miracles" (see Ps. 77:14); for Job, He is the Lord who can do all things (see Job 42:2); Daniel called Him the "Ancient of days" (Dan. 7:9); St. Paul revered Him as "the Name above other names" (see Phil. 2:9); St. Peter served Him as "the living Stone" (see 1 Pet. 1:4); St. John beheld Him as "the Lion of the tribe of Judah, the Root of David" (Rev. 5:5); and Jesus revealed Himself as "the root and the offspring of David, the bright morning star" (Rev. 22:16).

At those times when the thick clouds of evil begin to gather, when the smoke of Satan begins to blur our view and choke our breath, intercessors might opt to descend into the bright cloud of praise, invoking these awesome names, instead of a mournful prayer-fight. This kind of approach is a wonderful manifestation of faith. It means that one continues to trust God's powers and fidelity despite all odds and therefore joins with the perpetual praise of the angels and saints in heaven. In this way, the heavenly hosts are united in spiritual warfare. For the psalmist testifies in Psalm 8:2 (NIV): "Through the praise of children and infants you have established a stronghold against your enemies, to silence the foe and the avenger." This pattern of warfare could be seen in the exploits of King Jehoshaphat of Judah.

When King Jehoshaphat was under the threat of three kings bound by treaty, who summoned him to war, he exploited the weapon of praise. Instead of preparing an army for war he prepared a choir of praise. He instructed them to sing to the Lord and to praise Him for the splendor of His holiness. So, as they marched, they sang: "Give thanks to the Lord, for His love endures forever." This thunderous praise set the Lord to task, and the oracle of wisdom recounted: "And when they began to sing and praise, the Lord set an ambush against the men of Ammon, Moab, and Mount Seir, who had come against Judah, so that they were routed. For the men of Ammon and Moab rose against the inhabitants of Mount Seir, destroying them utterly, and when they had made an end of the inhabitants of Seir, they all helped to destroy one another" (2 Chron. 20:22–23).

When Shadrach, Meshach and Abednego[27] were thrown into the heart of the fire because of their rejection of idolatry, instead of asking God questions and dropping their heads in defeat, they

---

[27] Note that the original names of these young men were Hananiah, Mishael, and Azariah, before the chief official of Nebuchadnezzar changed them to Shadrach, Meshach and Abednego, respectively (Dan. 1:6).

took the way of King Jehoshaphat and offered God the gift of praise. The description of this scenario in the book of Daniel is very inspiring:

> They walked around in the midst of the flames, singing hymns to God and blessing the Lord. Then Azariah stood still in the fire and prayed aloud: "Blessed are you, O Lord, God of our ancestors, and worthy of praise; and glorious is your name forever! For you are just in all you have done; all your works are true and your ways right, and all your judgments are true." (Dan. 3:24–27, NRSVCE)

Heaven could not resist this soulful praise and therefore responded by sending down into the fire "someone like the Son of Man." When the divine figure came into the heart of the fire to make them four persons, the tempo of praise changed. It then became chants of praise that transformed their fire into an instrument of worship. For the fourth man in the fire, presumably an angel, drove the fiery flame out of the furnace, and made the inside of the furnace as though a moist wind were whistling through it. Scripture puts this glorious praise worship this way:

> Then the three with one voice praised and glorified and blessed God in the furnace: "Blessed are you, O Lord, God of our ancestors, and to be praised and highly exalted forever; and blessed is your glorious, holy name, and to be highly praised and highly exalted forever. Blessed are you in the temple of your holy glory, and to be extolled and highly glorified forever. Blessed are you who look into the depths from your throne on the cherubim, and to be praised and highly exalted forever. Blessed are you on the throne of your kingdom, and to be extolled and

highly exalted forever. Blessed are you in the firmament of heaven, and to be sung and glorified forever. Bless the Lord, all you works of the Lord; sing praise to Him and highly exalt Him forever. Bless the Lord, you heavens; sing praise to Him and highly exalt Him forever. Bless the Lord, you angels of the Lord; sing praise to Him and highly exalt Him forever. Bless the Lord, all you waters above the heavens; sing praise to Him and highly exalt Him forever. Bless the Lord, all you powers of the Lord; sing praise to Him and highly exalt Him forever." (Dan. 3:51–61, NRSVCE)

The effect of this praise worship was not only that the three young men were not consumed in the furnace. It also brought a tremendous miracle of conversion and salvation. For King Nebuchadnezzar, after witnessing this miracle, said: "Therefore I make a decree: Any people, nation, or language that utters blasphemy against the God of Shadrach, Meshach, and Abednego shall be torn limb from limb, and their houses laid in ruins; for there is no other god who is able to deliver in this way'" (Dan. 3:96, NRSVCE).[28]

Paul and Silas also exploited the power of praise when they were arrested for the sake of the name of Jesus and thrown into prison (see Acts 16). One would have expected that after they had been humiliated, stripped, and beaten with rods at the order of a Roman magistrate, sustained wounds, and finally incarcerated with criminals, these two soldiers of Christ would have been discouraged or engaged in sending petitions asking for help from

---

[28] Note that this part of Scripture, that is, the full story of these three young men, is not contained in Protestant editons of the Bible. It can be found only in Catholic Bibles.

heaven. They did none of these but rather joined in the praise. They clapped, sang, and praised the name of their ever-faithful God. Their chains—for they were in chains—as they were clapping and dancing, became for them tambourines and cymbals, harmonizing their music into a sweet melody. And that was the hammer. God came down with great might to receive praise but not without pressing home His character—deliverance, and a miracle: "And suddenly there was a great earthquake, so that the foundations of the prison were shaken; and immediately all the doors were opened and every one's fetters were unfastened" (Acts: 16:26).

The Church on earth, the militant Church, has this great insight about the power of praise and organizes her liturgy in such a way that it unites with the Church in heaven, the triumphant Church, in this perpetual adoration of the Lord. The greatest act of worship she gives God is the Holy Mass. In the early part of this sacred celebration, the Church, gathered in worship, chants the Gloria. This is a song the Church sings with vibrating joy and to the instruments of music as it worships its Lord and Master. This worship continues in praise and thanksgiving through the whole of the Eucharistic celebration but reaches its climax at the Consecration. To conclude the celebration, the priest says to the congregation, "Go in the peace of Christ," and the people of God respond, "Thanks be to God." Worshippers leave the temple of the Lord with thanksgiving on their lips.

It is indeed true that God made us for His glory, and the Church acknowledges this and makes her life accordingly a total praise. The Liturgy of the Hours is equally constituted basically to be diverse chants of praise drawn from the psalms and canticles in the Bible. Although it also contains readings and petitions for different occasions, its basic undertone is praise and worship.

An instance could be taken from the prayer that is known as the Te Deum.[29] It is a relatively long but beautiful prayer of praise, worship, and thanksgiving:

We praise You, O God: we acclaim You as the Lord.
Everlasting Father, all the world bows down before You.
All angels sing Your praise, the hosts of heaven and all the
angelic powers: all the Cherubim and Seraphim call to You
in unending song: Holy, holy, holy, is the Lord God of
angel hosts! The heavens and the earth are filled with Your
majesty and glory. The glorious band of apostles, the noble
company of prophets, the white-robed army who shed their
blood for Christ, all sing Your praise. And to the ends of the
earth, Your holy Church proclaims her faith in You: Father,
whose majesty is boundless, Your true and only son, who
is to be adored, the Holy Spirit sent to be our advocate.
You Christ are the king of glory, Son of the eternal Father.
When You took our nature to save mankind, You did not
shrink from birth in the Virgin womb. You overcame the
power of death, opening the Father's kingdom to all who
believe in You. Enthroned at God's right hand in the glory
of the Father, You will come in judgment according to Your
promise. You redeemed Your people by Your precious blood.
Come, we implore You, to our aid. Grant us with the
saints a place in eternal glory Lord, save Your people and
bless Your inheritance. Rule them and uphold them for-

---

[29] This is an early Christian hymn of praise known as the Ambrosian Hymn or the Song of the Church. The title Te Deum is taken from its opening Latin words, *Te Deum laudamus*, translated as "Thee, O God, we praise."

*ever and ever. Day by day we praise You: we acclaim You
now and for all eternity. In Your goodness, Lord, keep us
free from sin. Have mercy on us, Lord, have mercy. May
your mercy always be with us, Lord, for we have hoped in
you. In you, Lord we put our trust: we shall not be put to
shame.*

The life of the Church is indeed saturated with praise and
worship. The Lord said, "When I am lifted up, you will know
that I am He" (see John 8:28). "And I, when I am lifted up from
the earth, will draw all people to myself" (John 12:32, NIV).
Though these texts are fundamentally the Lord's prophetic words
referring to His Crucifixion, they can be figuratively understood
in the sense of lifting Him up with praise and worship. He loves
being lifted up in this manner. He accomplishes great works
when His children lift Him up with praise, and the Church
knows this truth.

It is necessary that intercessors learn the role of praise in their
ministry from our Mother, the Church. They should possess the
praise of God on their lips without letting go of their double-
edged swords, since their hands have been trained for battle
and their arms for war (see Ps. 144:1). A vigil of praise could be
organized in which God is lifted high all night. It is the duty of
believers to praise Him with hymns, musical instruments of all
kinds, clapping and dancing as the Spirit gives inspiration. For
the psalmist says: "Sing joyfully to the Lord, you righteous; it is
fitting for the upright to praise Him. Praise the Lord with the
harp; make music to Him on the ten-stringed lyre. Sing to Him
a new song; play skillfully, and shout for joy" (Ps. 33:1–3, NIV).
It is truly good to praise the Lord. This can greatly enhance the
intercessory exploits of an intercessor.

The Name of Jesus

There is something in the name of Jesus that is awesome and fascinating. Hence, the quiver of an intercessor cannot be complete without it. The name of Jesus is the seat of authority. St. Paul highlights the power that is intrinsically connected with this name when he says: "Therefore God has highly exalted Him and bestowed on Him the name which is above every name, that at the name of Jesus every knee should bow, in heaven and on earth and under the earth, and every tongue confess that Jesus Christ is Lord, to the glory of God the Father" (Phil. 2:9–11). An invocation of this name in faith will activate the power in it to save. The kingdom of darkness is sent trembling and confused when this wonderful name is invoked. The demons shudder at the mention of the name Jesus.

St. Peter the fisherman, who served Jesus very faithfully, knows better what this name constitutes. While he and John were going to the Temple to pray, a cripple asked alms from them. Peter said to him: "I have no silver and gold, but I give you what I have; in the name of Jesus Christ of Nazareth, walk" (Acts 3:6). The crippled man sprang up instantly and walked. They were thereafter arrested for using the name of Jesus to perform a miracle. The elders and rulers of the people thought that they had done away with Jesus, but His disciples made them understand that He was still present through His awesome name. During the process of interrogation, Peter, filled with the Holy Spirit, told them: "Be it known to you all, and to all the people of Israel, that by the name of Jesus Christ of Nazareth, whom you crucified, whom God raised from the dead, by Him this man is standing before you well. This is the stone which was rejected by you builders, but which has become the head of the corner. And there is salvation in no one else, for there is no other name under heaven given among men by which we must be saved" (Acts 4:10–12).

Jesus declares to John the Evangelist: "I Jesus have sent my angel to you with this testimony for the churches. I am the root and the offspring of David, the bright morning star" (Rev. 22:16). David is the symbol of authority in Israel. To talk about the dynasty of Israel is to talk about the dynasty of David. He is the reference point and the seat of power and authority in subsequent dynasties in Israel and Judah. But Jesus acknowledges that He is the root of this authority. He is the meaning and the soul of this Davidic authority. It was in Him that the successful exploits of David were rooted. This explains the prophecy of Isaiah when he said: "For to us a child is born, to us a son is given; and the government will be upon His shoulder, and His name will be called Wonderful Counselor, Mighty God, Everlasting Father, Prince of Peace. Of the increase of His government and of peace there will be no end, upon the throne of David, and over His kingdom" (Isa. 9:6–7).

This is to say that it is Jesus who determines the status of every other kingdom, earthly or spiritual. Every form of government is rooted in Him: the government of spirits and of men, of angels and of demons, of nature and of the supernatural. The nonspecification of this government in the text quoted from the prophet Isaiah shows that His authority is all encompassing. For "in Him we live and move and have our being" (Acts. 17:28). And apart from Him we can do nothing (John 15:5). Since He has the key of David (Rev. 3:7), He has access to unassailable authority. Thus, in the name of Jesus resides all the divinity of God, the power that raised Him from the dead:

> He is the image of the invisible God, the first-born of all creation; for in Him all things were created, in heaven

and on earth, visible and invisible, whether thrones or dominions or principalities or authorities—all things were created through Him and for Him. He is before all things, and in Him all things hold together. He is the head of the body, the Church; He is the beginning, the first-born from the dead, that in everything He might be pre-eminent. For in Him all the fullness of God was pleased to dwell. (Col. 1:15–19)

And for Him to be the root and at the same time the offspring of David means that He was, He is, and He will continue to be the Alpha and the Omega (Rev. 1:8). His authority is both universal and eternal. Accordingly, the letter to the Hebrews testifies: "Jesus Christ is the same yesterday and today and forever" (13:8). Thus, when we speak about the name of Jesus, we speak about the authority that is connected with the Person of Jesus. It is for this reason that He told His disciples: "And these signs will accompany those who believe: in my name they will cast out demons; they will speak in new tongues; they will pick up serpents; and if they drink any deadly thing, it will not hurt them; they will lay their hands on the sick, and they will recover" (Mark 16:17–18). The victory of believers over evil is rooted in the name of Jesus.

There was this case of a young girl who was attacked in a dream by demonic forces. The next morning she discovered that she had lost her power of speech. The condition defied medical diagnosis and treatment. This trouble lingered for a week before some intercessors took up the case. At a point in the prayer of intervention, she was asked to pronounce the name of Jesus. It was difficult. She was encouraged to do it while intercessions continued. She tried harder and harder but did not succeed. She was made to understand what authority this name bore and exhorted to step out in faith and fill her mind with the power in this name and use her mental strength to move her tongue to pronounce the name of Jesus. She took a step of faith and tried again and again, and all of a sudden she shouted, "Jeeeesssuuuuuusss."

And that was it. The yoke was broken and the miracle happened. In the name of Jesus every knee shall bow.

No one can make demons subject to him except with the name of Jesus. Thus, Justin Martyr stated with pride and authority:

> For every demon, when exorcised in the name of this very Son of God — who is the First-born of every creature, who became man by the Virgin, who suffered, and was crucified under Pontius Pilate by your nation, who died, who rose from the dead, and ascended into heaven — is overcome and subdued. But though you exorcise any demon in the name of any of those who were amongst you — either kings, or righteous men, or prophets, or patriarchs — it will not be subject to you.[30]

It does not take much to call the name of Jesus. Only a guileless believing tongue can do it. Just call it from the depth of your being with a faith devoid of doubt. Intercessors should discover this power and exploit it. Christians, who know this, have used it to score lots of victories. Since my secondary school days, I have loved this beautiful song from the little hymn book called "Ancient and Modern," even before I began to experience its contents in praxis:

---

[30] Justin Martyr, *Dialogue with Trypho* 85.

How sweet the name of Jesus sounds in a believer's
ear.
It soothes his sorrows, heals his wounds, and drives
away his fear.
It makes the wounded spirit whole, and calms the
troubled breast;
'Tis manna to the hungry soul, and to the weary, rest.

The Blood of Jesus

The blood of Jesus, like His name, is another source of strength
and power for believers. An intercessor can use it effectively in
his intercessory mission. When war broke out in heaven, and
Satan was defeated, he was thrown down to the earth with his
angels. Then a voice reported that they were overcome by the
blood of the Lamb and the word of the testimony of the servants
of God (see Rev. 12:11).

Blood signifies the vital force of an animal, for the life of an
animal is in its blood (see Lev. 17:11). The Bible uses it to refer
to the vital principle of an animal. It then means the source of
energy and strength of an animal to live and accomplish its un-
dertakings. That is why when a person sheds his blood on behalf
of anything or anybody, it is seen as a supreme sacrifice, and it
is expected that this sacrifice will produce greater fruits for the
cause for which the person died. It is against this background
that the shedding of the blood of a Christian for the sake of his
faith in Christ has been considered a blessing for Christianity.
Thus, the pouring out of one's blood for the glory of God, when
necessitated, is a supreme oblation, a martyrdom.

However, one who also suffered for the sake of Christ and
died for the sake of what he believes about Christ, though he

may not have shed physical blood, can also be called a martyr. Martyrdom in itself could be essentially understood as a conquest of Satan. The martyr has proved superior to every seduction and to every threat and even to the violence of Satan. Here is a dramatic truth of life—every time we choose to suffer rather than be disloyal to God, it is the defeat of Satan.[31]

Now, if the spilling of the blood of a martyr, literally and indirectly, is the defeat of Satan, then the pouring out of the blood of Jesus should be the summary of the defeat of Satan—any further defeat of Satan is only a continuation of this once-and-for-all defeat of Satan through the blood of the Lamb.

The sight or the mere invocation of the blood of Jesus has always terrorized the devil. It reminds him of the great and crushing defeat he suffered on Good Friday, which culminated in the Crucifixion on Mount Calvary. Whenever the blood is invoked, it not only replays for him the events of the Cross but also makes it actual. It reminds him of the event that unseated him; the event that snatched his key of operation and oppression; the event that wrecked his kingdom and thrust his army into disarray; the event that humiliated him and put him under a believer's authority; and the event that made him a perpetual loser. This is the experience he detests with utmost loathing and would never wish to have again. But the invocation of the blood of Jesus reviews all this with all its devastating effects, if it is done by clean lips and with faith.

The power in the blood of the Lamb is most effectively released during the Eucharistic celebration. In this celebration, as already discussed, the events of Calvary are relived, and souls are purchased for God once again. The slaying of the Lamb is

---

[31] Barclay, *The Daily Study Bible*, p. 123.

reenacted at every Holy Mass, and through the blood of the slain Lamb men are ransomed for God from every tribe and people and nation (see Rev. 5:9). Whenever and wherever there is the need to purchase men again for God, the invocation of this blood will accomplish it. Its powers have a far-reaching effect.

Let us go through the prophecy in chapter 47 of the book of Ezekiel and become acquainted with the mystical meaning of Ezekiel's vision in relation to Calvary and the blood of the Lamb. Ezekiel was led by a man in a vision in which he saw a temple. He noticed that water was flowing from the southern part of that temple. That water continued to collect together and increase in volume until it became a river no one could walk across. This water flowed down into the River Araba, from where it entered the sea. When it emptied into the sea, the water in the sea became fresh. There would emerge a large number of fish because this water flowed there and made the saltwater fresh. So, wherever the river flowed, everything would live. Fruit trees of all kinds would grow on both banks of the river. The leaves would not wither, nor would their fruits fail. Every month the trees would bear fruits because the water from the sanctuary flowed to them. Their fruits were to serve as food and their leaves for healing.

This was a vision of an event that was yet to take place, and it was revealed to Ezekiel. Put in another way, Ezekiel saw a temple and water flowing from its southern part. This water refreshed every other water it flowed into. This same water brought life and restoration while it flowed along. It brought consistent productivity, including fruits and leaves that provided food for the hungry and healing for the sick. How could this vision be understood? What is the interpretation? This part of the Old Testament helps to highlight the fact that while the

New Testament is the fulfillment of the Old Testament, the Old Testament is the prefiguration of the New Testament—they complement each other.

We recall that when the Jews accosted Jesus and asked Him to give them a sign that would authenticate His authority for doing all that He was doing, He told them, "Destroy this temple, and in three days I will raise it up" (John 2:19). Because their eyes were too dull to understand Scripture, the Jews thought He was referring to the Temple of Jerusalem and retorted: "It has taken forty-six years to build this temple, and will you raise it up in three days?" (John 2:20). The evangelist then added a statement that makes a great difference: "But He spoke of the temple of His body" (John 2:21). Here Jesus called Himself the "temple." Now, when the Jews unwittingly accepted the advice of Jesus, they took Him to the place of the Skull and hanged Him on a tree. In this way they destroyed the temple. Then, "one of the soldiers pierced His side with a spear, and at once there came out blood and water" (John 19:34). This is the unfolding fulfillment of the vision of Ezekiel. Jesus was the temple in this vision. His wounded side, from which water and blood flowed, is the southern side of the temple in the vision. The blood and water flowing from the pierced side are represented by the water flowing from the southern part of the temple in Ezekiel's vision. Hundreds of years before the death of Jesus, Ezekiel saw in a vision the event and its effects.

Note that the Bible calls the water flowing from the temple in the vision of Ezekiel the "river of life." It has a lot of beautiful effects. It purifies the sea into which it flows. It brings productivity and cures barrenness. It is the spring of abundance. It offers hope for the weary, food for the hungry, and healing for the sick. It has a reviving and refreshing effect. It never dries up and leads the way to everlasting life because it continues to flow until it empties into the sea. The water guarantees perpetuity because it is not obstructed but flows continuously.

The vision of Ezekiel is thus a vision that enlightens us about the refreshing power of the blood of the Lamb. It cleanses and washes brighter than snow. It purifies sinners who make them-selves available to it. When intercessors plead for mercy, this blood, which pleads more insistently for mercy than the blood of Abel pleads for vengeance (see Heb. 12:24), is available. There is always a copious flow of this blood. It is always enough for ev-ery case. Like Ezekiel's river of life, which prefigured this blood, it gives new life and refreshment. This is what the Lord meant when He said through the prophet Ezekiel, "I will sprinkle clean water upon you, and you shall be clean from all your unclean-nesses, and from all your idols I will cleanse you. A new heart I will give you, and a new spirit I will put within you; and I will take out of your flesh the heart of stone and give you a heart of flesh" (Ezek. 36:25–26).

Note, however, this interesting statement in Ezekiel's vision: "But its swamps and marshes will not become fresh; they are to be left for salt" (Ezek. 47:11). There are areas and things the water does not purify or make fresh. This is but for a purpose — so that there would be salt, a very important element for human survival. This helps us to understand that when the blood of the Lamb seems not to have achieved our desired end, even though it was invoked with faith and by guileless lips, it is for a purpose. We may not know for what purpose, but with faith we must trust that it is in order that salt may be made available.

The writer of the letter to the Hebrews says, Jesus is "the same yesterday and today and forever" (Heb. 13:8). Thus, the effect of His mission on the Cross yesterday is still fresh and efficacious today and will remain so forever. Christ's blood is still flowing down from His wounded "fountain" and will ever continue. His wounds "never heal." If they do, He will no longer heal us, for it is by those wounds that we are healed (see Isa. 53:5).[32] Accordingly, the river of life has continued to flow. Yesterday the River Jordan was a river of healing for the leprous Naaman; today something greater than the River Jordan is here. Yesterday there was the pool of healing at Bethesda (house of mercy); today something greater than the Bethesda pool is here. It is the great pool of the blood of the immolated Lamb. Ezekiel saw it in a vision, and the river Jordan and the pool of Bethesda prefigured it. Whoever goes to the foot of the Cross and comes under the bleeding Messiah for healing, for cleansing, and for an answer to petitions, is sure to be abundantly satisfied. Intercessors should take up the duty of transporting their clients to this beautiful River of Life.

This precious blood, which is the gift from Calvary and the root of our Christian faith, is the pride of the Church. The Church celebrates it with joy every day of her life in the Eucharist. By this, the event of Calvary is reenacted and perpetuated. Through it this ineffable blood continues to flow from one generation to the next.

The Fire of the Holy Spirit

It appears funny seeing some believers in some parts of the world gather and fill the air with chants of thunderous "Holy Ghost Fire." People ask, "Who introduced this Holy Ghost Fire thing? Is this not making a caricature of the Holy Spirit? This is surely

---

[32] This must not be understood literally but in its mystical sense.

unorthodox." Although the use of this apparently novel cliché might sound crazy and funny, we should first ascertain whether this is just a hysterico-emotional outburst signifying nothing or whether it really produces any spiritual effects that qualify it as one of the arrows needed in the quiver of an intercessor.

God was repeatedly identified with fire in the Old Testament. In the New Testament, He is also profusely associated with fire. The psalmist says that fire prepares His path (see Ps. 97:3), while the letter to the Hebrews calls Him "a Consuming Fire" (Heb. 12:29). He has often answered His people through fire. On one occasion, in the days God used Moses to punish Egypt with a series of plagues, Moses stretched out his rod toward heaven, and the Lord sent thunder and hail, and fire came down on the earth (see Exod. 9:23). When David offered a sin offering, praying the Lord to end the plague that was nearly wiping out the entire population of Israel, fire came down and consumed his sacrifice (see 1 Chron. 21:26). As Solomon offered his sacrifice during the dedication of the Temple of Jerusalem, God answered, consuming the sacrifice with fire (see 2 Chron. 7:1). Elijah had the same experience on Mount Carmel when he contested with the prophets of Baal (see 1 Kings 18:38). He specifically invoked God to answer by fire. The response was instantaneous. It is therefore not wrong for a believer to make use of this provision responsibly and invoke the God who answers by fire.

The fire of the Holy Spirit could be used as both an offensive and a defensive weapon. It is like the word of God, which is double-edged and therefore dual in purpose. The experience of the people of Israel in Egypt and while traveling to the promised land shows how this fire could serve as a source of divine protection. While they were on the way to the promised land "the Lord went in front of them in a pillar of cloud by day, to lead them, along the way, and in a pillar of fire by night, to give them light, so that they might travel by day and by night (see Exod. 13:21). Accordingly, the Master promised in the book of the prophet Zechariah: "For I will be to her a wall of fire round about" (2:5). Again, when the Assyrian army was poised against Elisha, it was an army of angels with flaming swords that surrounded him for protection.

Elijah made profuse use of this holy fire as an offensive weapon when he was threatened by King Ahaziah of Israel (2 Kings 1). Ahaziah committed idolatry when he sent messengers to Ekron to consult Baalzebub and inquire if he would survive his sickness. God felt despised and sent Elijah, His own messenger, therefore, to go and meet the messengers of Ahaziah with the message: "'Is it because there is no God in Israel that you are going to inquire of Baalzebub, the god of Ekron?' Now therefore thus says the Lord, 'You shall not come down from the bed to which you have gone, but you shall surely die'" (2 Kings 1:3–4). Instead of receiving the message of God with trembling and compunction, the king sent a captain with fifty soldiers to go and arrest Elijah.[33]

The captain and his men visited Elijah, who was on the top of a hill. Probably Elijah went back to prayer after visiting the messengers of Ahaziah. The hill or mountain was the common place where men of God spent time with their Lord in prayer. Elijah was seasoned in spiritual warfare and knew that the devil should not be given any breathing space; otherwise he would do evil. He knew that Ahaziah was an evil king and consequently

---

[33] This passage should be read with a deeper spiritual insight. It should be understood as a metaphorical representation of a spiritual warfare.

understood that whenever there is an action, there must be a reaction. So, he went back to wait for the backlash of wickedness. An intercessor must be ready at all times, especially after such encounters that would necessarily upset the enemy. It is always disastrous when the evil one takes an intercessor unawares. This has been the undoing of many believers and especially intercessors—complacency, sleeping on duty.

But Elijah knew better.

The captain yelled his command at Elijah, "O man of God, the king says, 'Come down.'" The captain and his men were armed and equipped with the authority of the king. This gave the captain the audacity to give Elijah orders and to attempt to intimidate him. Intercessors should beware of such tricks of the enemy, who uses fear to disarm his opponents. He roars like a lion but, in fact, is not a lion. Compared to the authority and arsenal of powers at the disposal of believers, he is rather a mouse with a microphone. They should not be afraid to go out to face him. An intercessor must always know the ground on which he stands—a solid rock, Christ the Lord. He must know the stuff of the arrows in his quiver. He must never forget that he is a polished arrow fashioned by the greatest craftsman, the Lord of hosts, and concealed in His quiver (see Isa. 49:2). Elijah was such an experienced messenger of the Lord of hosts.

Consequently, he had no time for compromise or pleasantries. He pulled the trigger immediately: "If I am a man of God, let fire come down from heaven and consume you and your fifty." He too was serving not just a king but the King of kings and was equally on the mission of his Master. He possessed his own authority from his own King to give orders. For according to the prophecy of Isaiah, "He made my mouth like a sharp sword, in the shadow of His hand He hid me; He made me a polished arrow, in His quiver He hid me away" (Isa. 49:2). God has put His word in the mouth of an intercessor and covered him with the shadow of His hand (see Isa. 51:16). He needs only to open his mouth and make decrees.

The way Ahaziah responded to the message of God made it seem as if he was challenging the authority of the Master. He seemed to have instituted a war between the king of Israel and the King of kings. God thus decided to teach him a lesson. It then came to pass that as soon as the command left the lips of Elijah, "fire came down from heaven, and consumed him and his fifty."

The use of Holy Ghost fire is, in effect, a reproduction of what Elijah did on the hill. What Elijah did here is one of the uses of the Holy Ghost fire. When we feel threatened by evil, it is a sacred act to invoke this sacred fire as both an offensive and a defensive weapon. The quiver of an intercessor may remain incomplete without this arrow.

The fire of the Holy Spirit could also be appealed to for purification, renewal, or empowerment. For this reason, the Church prays: "Come, O Holy Spirit! Fill the hearts of the faithful and enkindle in them the fire of Your love." It brings conversion even to the hardest of souls. It can turn hearts on for God. It is a wonderful act of charity to plead with the Third Person of the Blessed Trinity to descend with His fire and invade any territory that does not honor God and transform it into a source of glory for God. When Christians are commissioned for service as members of the Lord's army, the worshipping community of God also invokes this fire for empowerment through its anointing.

This fire must, however, not be used incautiously or with an ungodly intention. That would be an abuse of its purpose and a discourtesy to the Holy Spirit. For it to produce its effects, it must be invoked responsibly. It should never be intended directly or indirectly against human beings perceived as enemies but rather used when we are engaged in spiritual battles with evil forces. When it is used against men who practice witchcraft or people who run errands for the devil, directly or indirectly, the fire must be directed against their source of power and evil practices and not against their persons. The invocation of this fire is ultimately intended to set captives free and stop the devil from wreaking further havoc. Even those men and women who are in the service of the devil are also sons and daughters of Abraham for whom Jesus shed His blood and therefore are equally in need of salvation. They are among the souls an intercessor is fighting to bring back home to the Father. So He cannot intend to destroy that for which He is on a rescue mission.

It is noteworthy that when the Samaritans refused Jesus passage through their town, James and John wanted to call down fire to destroy them (Luke 9:54).[34] James and John knew they were capable of bringing down fire and wanted to use this power with the permission of the Master. Jesus knew too that they could bring down fire — they were His disciples and were already learning from their Master. But He needed to use this opportunity to teach them about the responsible use of the holy fire that comes from heaven. Thus, He rebuked them immediately and disabused their minds from thinking of such evil against their fellow men. He made them realize that this fire should not be used erratically or whimsically. Invoking fire for destruction is not meant against human beings but against forces of darkness.

---

[34] Perhaps that was the reason they were nicknamed the "sons of thunder."

Fasting

In the quiver of an intercessor there is a very important place for fasting. Fasting has been part of the spirituality of the people of God since Old Testament times. Jesus used it as a mighty weapon to enter spiritual warfare. This shows that the principles guiding the participation of Christians in the divine council and of being active participants in the events going on in the spiritual realm remain, to date, unaltered. Spiritual warfare was declared as early as the origin of the human species and has continued ever since. All who have engaged in this battle have recognized fasting as a veritable spiritual weapon.

The Lord also demands fasting as a means of restoring friendship with Him after separation caused by sin. He spoke to His people in the book of the prophet Joel: "Return to me with all your heart, with fasting, with weeping, and with mourning; and rend your hearts and not your garments" (2:12–13).

Fasting humbles the body and liberates the soul to communicate with God. The Lenten Eucharistic Prayer IV reads: "For through bodily fasting you restrain our faults, raise up our minds, and bestow both virtue and its rewards, through Christ our Lord." Many men and women of God employed the spiritual weapon of fasting in their encounters with God. We will, however, select a few salient ones here to illustrate the place of fasting in the mission of an intercessor.

The prophet Nehemiah was given an unfavorable report about the Jews who survived the exile in Persia and the condition of Jerusalem, the city of David, in about 445 B.C. The report reads: "The survivors there in the province who escaped exile are in great trouble and shame; the wall of Jerusalem is broken down, and its gates are destroyed by fire" (Neh. 1:3). Nehemiah became very sad and troubled. But he remembered the covenant God made with His people and recalled that God was full of mercy and love, abounding in forgiveness. He decided to intercede for his people, Israel. He wept and fasted for days in the presence of the God of heaven. The Lord gave ear to his groaning. He was granted the favor to lead the remnant of Israel back to their land and to rebuild Jerusalem.

Ezra used the same means to attract God's mercies for the returning Jewish survivors when they were ready to get back to their land from Persia. Ezra reported:

> Then I proclaimed a fast there, at the river Ahava that we might humble ourselves before our God, to seek from Him a straight way for ourselves, our children, and all our goods. For I was ashamed to ask the king for a band of soldiers and horsemen to protect us against the enemy on our way; since we had told the king, "The hand of our God is for good upon all that seek Him, and the power of His wrath is against all that forsake Him." So we fasted and besought our God for this, and He listened to our entreaty. (Ezra 8:21–23)

Daniel also made use of fasting to get the attention of heaven during Israel's exile in Babylon. He fasted for three weeks until heaven responded.

Queen Esther employed this arrow, too, when Israel was threatened with extinction while in exile. In order to meet King Ahasuerus, whose presence would not be approached without invitation unless one wished execution, and convince him to cancel the edict that had already been signed to exterminate all the Jewish people in his vast kingdom, Esther fasted and demanded the same from her people. She told her uncle Mordecai: "Go, gather all the Jews to be found in Susa, and hold a fast on my behalf, and neither eat nor drink for three days, night or day. I and my maids will also fast as you do. Then I will go to the king, though it is against the law; and if I perish, I perish" (Esther 4:16). Her petition was heard, and Israel was miraculously saved.

Jesus Himself began His mission with a forty-day and -night fast. It is very clear how greatly He succeeded. He taught His disciples the importance of fasting in spiritual warfare. Once, the apostles could not drive out a dumb and deaf demon from its victim. They wondered why they could not do that and why the demon refused to obey their commands. Jesus enlightened them after He had expelled the demon and said, "This kind can come forth by nothing, but by prayer and fasting" (Mark 9:29, KJV).

Christian spirituality considers fasting a bedrock. An uncountable number of the children of the Church dedicated their lives to fasting and penance. Some of them went into the deserts and secluded areas to live as hermits. Asceticism was thus a common practice among the saints gone before us. That was the reason many of them personally encountered God and brought down many divine favors here on earth. St. Anthony of Egypt said: "The demons dread the ascetics' fast." A mortified life lifts up a soul and adorns it. Asceticism frees the soul to journey and actively participate in the divine council.

An ascetic is a disciplined, self-controlled man. He is frugal with words, food, and the use of the senses. He reins in his thoughts and emotions from straying. He therefore stands above others with a generous spiritual output.

Consider the asceticism of Jesus. If Jesus were not already disciplined by asceticism, I wonder how much He would have resisted the devil's intrigues. The devil tempted Him with three basic human inclinations: food and drink, wealth, and honor. If anyone wishes to be nourished by the intercessory powers of the Lord, he must first triumph over these inclinations. Fasting is therefore not just about forgoing food and drink. It demands the frugal use of the senses and the restraint of the body from some pleasures in order to humble it for a greater spiritual harvest.

This does not, however, mean that the body should be harshly denied all the necessities of life or that one should intentionally hurt one's health while on an intercessory mission. What is being encouraged here is the need to discipline the body (self) so that it can cooperate with the spirit while it journeys to participate in the divine council.

When Daniel interceded for his people, his three weeks' fast was notably not dry. He depended on some food and drink: "In those days I, Daniel, was mourning for three weeks. I ate no delicacies, no meat or wine entered my mouth, nor did I anoint myself at all, for the full three weeks" (Dan. 10:2–3).

If an intercessor fasts, it must be to the limit that he can still have enough strength to pray and in accordance with his health conditions. It is most advisable to fast from choice foods and drinks, as Daniel did. This humbles the body more.

The ascetic life of an intercessor should equally not make him look haggard and unkempt. He should not appear shabby and dirty because of his self-denial. It is the teaching of our Lord that when we fast, we should wash our face and comb our hair. For this reason, St. Teresa of Avila prayed that God should save us from gloomy saints.

Thus, mortification should be rational and moderate, for to be holy is to be human. Spirituality without wisdom is empty and unproductive.

Our Lady's Psalter: The Holy Rosary

The Rosary always has been and always will be a very strong arrow in the quiver of an intercessor. It has often played the role of snatching a decadent age from the divine wrath. It has a sweet and swift way of reaching and moving the heart of the Lord.

God, who is rich in mercy, has a miraculous way of saving the people He ransomed at the pain of the blood of His Son. He has often used the mother of Jesus the Savior to intervene in human history and misery. She is a precious pearl God has given to humanity as a mother and intercessor. Her power of intervention, apart from her agreeing to be the ark of the new covenant, was first seen at the wedding at Cana in Galilee. When she noticed that the wine of the wedding hosts had finished, she was very concerned that they would be facing a terrible embarrassment. So she went to her Son and said, "They have no wine" (John 2:3). Although the Master remonstrated that His time had not yet come to be revealed, He could not refuse the request of His mother. Consequently He performed His first miracle and turned water into wine. This is the way our Lady has intervened in human history to help in times of difficulty.

Tradition holds that the virgin mother of God introduced the wonderful prayer called the Rosary (also known as the chaplet or Our Lady's Psalter) in its present form to St. Dominic in 1214 as a powerful means of directing the Albigensian heretics, known also as the Cathari, and other sinners back to the true Faith.

St. Dominic was very solicitous about the precarious fate of the heretic Albigensians and the devastating consequences of their error on the Christian faith. The Church authorities at the time did not help matters by using the Crusaders, military actions, and later the Inquisition to combat the problem. Dominic therefore withdrew from a world roasting in sin into a forest near

Toulouse in France, where he was engaged in a three-day agonizing prayer with harsh penance to appease the anger of God. He used this discipline so much that his body became lacerated. He finally fell into a trance in which he had a vision of our Lady. When he saw our Lady appear, accompanied by three angels, the following discussion ensued: "Dear Dominic, do you know which weapon the Blessed Trinity wants us to use to reform the world?" "O my Lady," answered the saint, "you know far better than I do because next to your son Jesus Christ you have always been the chief instrument of our salvation." Then our Lady replied, "I want you to know that, in this kind of warfare, the battering ram has always been the Angelic Psalter, which is the foundation stone of the New Testament. Therefore, if you want to reach these hardened souls and win them over to God, preach my psalter."[35]

Our Lady's psalter is composed of the angelic salutation: "Hail, O favored one, the Lord is with you! Blessed are you among women and blessed is the fruit of your womb!" (Luke 1:28, 42). It is this angelic salutation that resulted in Mary's fiat, which made our salvation possible. It is these biblical cornerstones of our salvation that have been finely organized into this prayer.

Meanwhile, St. Dominic took up the message of our Lady and preached the angelic psalter, and, true to our Lady's words, Albigensianism was finally defeated. From this time on, the Church has not failed to preach and to use the Rosary as a weapon of war and has experienced a series of glorious testimonies of the power of the Rosary, a few of which we would like to recall.

In 1945, during World War II, America dropped the first atomic bomb on Japan. This bomb exploded in Hiroshima, eight

---

[35] Father Aquinas, *The Holy Rosary* (Radium Springs, NM: Kingship of Christ Publishing, n.d.), p. 2.

city blocks from the Jesuit Church of Our Lady's Assumption. Half a million people were killed. All that was left was a thicket of darkness, blood, burns, moans, fire, and spreading clouds of terror. The church was also completely destroyed. However, the home attached to it, where eight Jesuit missionary Fathers lived and ministered to the Japanese people during the war, survived the atomic bomb. Not only did these priests all survive with (at most) relatively minor injuries; they all lived well past that awful day with no radiation sickness, no loss of hearing, and no other visible long-term defects or maladies. According to experts, "They ought to be dead." This miracle is attributed to the devotion of these priests to the Rosary of our Lady's Assumption. Fr. Schiffer, one of these survivors, said in one of their numerous interviews, "We believe that we survived because we were living the message of Fatima. We lived and prayed the Rosary daily in that home."[36]

Again, at the end of World War II, the allies did a nasty thing. They turned Catholic Austria over to the Russians, that is, marrying Catholicism and Communism. The Austrians tolerated this Soviet domination for three years, but that was enough. They wanted the Soviets out of their country. But what could they do, 7 million against 220 million?

It was at this time that the priest, Fr. Petrus, remembered Don John of Austria. Outnumbered three to one, Don John led the Papal Venetian and Spanish ships against the Muslim Turks at Lepanto, and through the power of the Rosary miraculously defeated them. So Fr. Petrus called for a Rosary crusade against the Soviets. He asked for a tithe: that 10 percent of the Austrians,

---

[36] "Famous Rosary Miracles," Miraculous Rosary, http://miraculousrosary.blogspot.com/p/famous-rosary-miracles.html.

700,000, would pledge to say the Rosary daily for the Soviets to leave their country. Seven hundred thousand pledged. For seven years the Austrians prayed the Rosary. Then, on May 13, 1955, the anniversary of the apparition at Fatima, the Russians left Austria. Even today, military strategists and historians are baffled by their sudden, unforeseen departure.[37]

Another miracle that testifies to the power of the Rosary was recorded in Brazil. In 1962, a deluge of communism was sweeping Brazil, as in Cuba. Fearing this turn to communism, Dona Amelia Bastos decided that it was time for the womenfolk of Brazil to take action. She therefore formed the Campaign of Women for Democracy. In Belo Horizonte, twenty thousand women reciting the Rosary aloud broke up the leftist meeting there. In Sao Paulo, six hundred thousand women praying the Rosary in one of the most moving demonstrations in Brazilian history sounded the deathknell there of the communist revolution.[38]

It has also been documented that the 1980s bloodless revolution, which ousted the despotic Ferdinand Marcos from power in the Philippines, was largely attributed to the praying of the Rosary.[39]

Our Lady, in her apparition in Fatima, promised the conversion of the Soviet Union if people would pray the Rosary. When the communist cancer turned so threatening, this plea of our

---

[37] Ibid.

[38] "Miracles of the Rosary: The Rosary Saves Brazil from Communism, 1962–1964," Catholic Go, April 1, 2015, http://catholicgo. org/miracles-of-the-rosary-the-rosary-saves-brazil-from-communism-1962-1964/.

[39] "Prayer Worked Miracles in the Philippines," FrTommyLane. com, http://www.frtommylane.com/stories/prayer/miracle_in_ the_philipines.htm.

Lady became most urgent. Rosary Crusades and Confraternities emerged in great numbers and with enthusiasm in many countries. Eventually the communist bloc of the Soviet Union was shattered.

The Rosary is a very violent storm against the powers of hell. It is always a celebration of the triumph of the Cross. It replays the devastating raid against the kingdom of darkness, and this is what the devil does not like to be reminded of. The Rosary is a sure means of torturing him with the memory of the woman who crushed and is still crushing his head (see Gen. 3:15). It is a wonderful prayer indeed, a sweet melody sung by believers and their queen about their history of salvation—from the Joyful Mysteries of the Annunciation, conception, and birth of Christ through the Sorrowful Mysteries of His agony on the Cross to the Glorious Mysteries of His Resurrection and Ascension into heaven and dovetailing with the mysteries of the dawn of the light of faith and salvation among nations.

These memories that are evoked during the recitation of the Rosary mercilessly torture the devil. It is little wonder then that he has embarked on an anti-Rosary crusade. Since the memory and presence of our Lady embarrasses, frustrates, and puts him to flight, he has engaged in a tireless job of sowing strong hatred against her in the souls of men. An event that took place in Canterbury Cathedral in 2017 is a strong pointer to the enemy's continued battle against Our Lady and her contributions to the salvation of man.

On February 18, 2017, Cardinal Nichols reconsecrated England and Wales to the Immaculate Heart of Mary in Westminster Cathedral. Surprisingly, on this same day, Justin Welby, the Church of England's Archbishop of Canterbury, was reported to have permitted a full Masonic service to be conducted in

Canterbury Cathedral, which was once the heart of the Catholic Church in England. The Voice for Global Orthodox Anglicanism reported that the archbishop decided to give permission after receiving a donation of almost $375,000 from the Masons for the restoration of the northwest transept in the Cathedral.[40]

The disturbing questions here are: Why did this Lodge decide to celebrate this rite on the same day of the reconsecration of England and Wales to our Lady, and why in a magnificent Christian cathedral, which used to be the mother of Catholic Churches in England? This incident highlights strongly the ongoing spiritual warfare, of which many seem ignorant. The devil is surely very afraid of our Lady and her interventions in the lives of men, and he struggles to fight back. He understands the spiritual effects of the act of reconsecration of England and Wales to our Lady and launches a counter ritual nearly on the same altar and on the same day. But our Lady remains the woman who crushes the head of the ancient serpent.

As another example, there was a demon that claimed to be the only true queen. This is not uncommon. The devil is known for such annoying arrogance. These are, however, empty boasts that signify nothing. When this demon refused to renounce this claim, a decision was taken by the deliverance team to bring in the true queen. Little more was done than the singing of some of her melodious hymns and the praying of the Hail Mary. This demon could not withstand this and began to shout: "No! Don't bring her into this matter. Tell her to go away. I don't want to

---

[40] Nick Donnelly, "Freemason Service at England's Mother Church on Same Day as Consecration to Our Lady," Church Militant, February 17, 2017, https://www.churchmilitant.com/news/article/freemason-service-at-englands-mother-church-on-same-day-as-consecration-to.

see her. Tell her to go away, and I shall settle with you." But the demon had to confess Mary's queenship and its own insignificance. The praying of the Hail Mary continued until the demon surrendered: "She is the queen. I am not!"

An intercessory team that does not have Mary as a matron and partner is short of an important arrow in its quiver. As far as Christianity is concerned, Mary remains the first and most powerful intercessor. It is recommended that an intercessor, as well as an intercessory group, should be dedicated to her. The testimony of a soul who was probably helped by the Vatican exorcist Gabriele Amorth is an eye-opener about the role of our Lady in the lives of those who fly to her for patronage. In his book *An Exorcist: More Stories*, Fr. Amorth publishes the personal story of this woman, which I will summarize here.

A demon began to torment the woman in 1974. Doctors and psychiatrists could not understand her strange conditions. Although she was a practicing Catholic who actively participated in her parish, she began to distance herself from the Catholic Church and disparage it every time the subject of religion came up. Her bitterness against the Church grew so strong that spending time in adoration in front of the Blessed Sacrament, which used to be a joy, became so boring that she wanted to run away from the Divine Presence. The entire Christian religious exercise appeared ridiculous to her, and she dismissed it as priestly theatrics and the idiocies of the faithful.

With time, she began to distance herself from the Church, started to associate with marginal groups, and sought exotic experiences. She studied astrology with passion and interpreted reality from the viewpoint of astrology and reincarnation. She subjected herself to hypnosis at the hands of a psychiatrist, who she learned had sworn a pact with Lucifer and pledged to destroy as many souls as possible. All these experiences and practices affected her physical health, too. Her body seemed to be in the grip of a vise. Her digestive system was blocked, her kidneys and joints malfunctioned, and she was always tired and listless. Her marriage and family were badly affected by these conditions.

She once had an occult experience that landed her in the hospital. The demon that was tormenting her followed her to the hospital, intending to destroy her. After two months, he influenced her to meddle with psychoanalysis and become a Buddhist. She practiced Zen meditation but felt disconnected and unhappy. She attended a school for teachers of yoga and began to teach hatha yoga in her village. At this point she felt a real hatred for the Church and cared about no one, not even about her husband and children.

In 1984 she had a miscarriage that resulted in surgery. But, in her own words, "The Lord was waiting for me at that hospital. He sent His Mother to comfort me. I felt the spiritual presence of the Virgin by my side, in my hospital room, helping me, reproaching me for my past, and inviting me to follow her. I felt so full of peace and light that I was happy to agree. This extraordinary experience brought me back to God." According to her, her parents had consecrated her as a child to the Virgin Mother of God. Mary's patronage eventually brought the woman to a priest, who helped her through to a complete exorcism.[41] The role of Our Lady in the lives of Christians should not be underestimated.

On another occasion, a prayer of deliverance was conducted for a seventeen-year-old boy who was possessed by twelve demons. It was a fierce battle. The boy was aggressive, and the power struggle was tough. At a point in this spiritual war, the boy

[41] Amorth, *An Exorcist*, pp. 51–55.

stopped his aggression suddenly, covered his face with one hand, and pointed in one direction with the other. "What is this?" He was shouting, "No! No!! No!!! My eyes are burning! Please, let somebody help me!" He invoked all the demons he knew, but to no avail. Nobody understood what was really happening until a rosary was discovered hanging on the wall, half-hidden by a calendar. It was this object that dazzled the boy's eyes and arrested his demonic powers—this sacramental that many dismiss as a fetish was producing the great effect that paralyzed the powers of the demons inhabiting the boy. Through a sacramental, God can dispense His grace just as He did with the bronze serpent of Moses (Num. 21:9), the shadow of Peter (Acts 5:15), and the handkerchiefs and aprons that touched St. Paul (Acts 19:12).

There was another encounter with an obdurate demon. When he had resisted many attacks, a rosary was flashed before his face. He was visibly shivering. At this instance he was asked, "Do you know what this is?" He said, "Yes!" "What is it?" "It is the weapon of the children of God," he answered. "Do you like it?" "No! No!! It is a very dangerous weapon," he cried. Even the demons confess the power of the Rosary.

The rosary is not a charm or amulet, as some choose to understand it, and, as such, view it with ignominy and hate. It is rather a treasure and a weapon of war. It is not meant to be worn for protection. Actually, its power does not reside merely in possessing it or in wearing it or hanging it on treasured possessions. Though its mere presence can create an aura of fear for the enemy and an air of divine presence, its actual power is in praying it and meditating on its divine mysteries.

Through the Rosary, believers ask our Lady for her intercession. They beseech her to do for them what she did for the wedding couple at Cana in Galilee. She has often intervened and helped obtain favors for those who fly to her patronage. It is for this reason that the Church calls her the Mediatrix of all graces.

A woman who had an issue of blood for three consecutive years came to a priest for help when no medical treatment could help her. She said that the problem started after she had her first baby. As a result of this condition, she could not have any further chance of conceiving again. The priest asked her to do two things for nine days: visit the Blessed Sacrament and the Marian shrine. He asked her to pray at least five decades of the Rosary each day at the Marian shrine. The woman informed the priest that she was a Protestant. The priest told her to pray according to her faith but made her understand that our Lady could help her in her prayers and encouraged her to visit a Marian shrine. She did. On the ninth and final day of her prayers, the priest laid hands on her, prayed for her, and blessed her. Her flow stopped the next day. One year later, she came back to the priest, heavy with child.

Praying the Rosary means praying with Mary. But some erroneously think that it is a multiplication of prayers and therefore pharisaic. They reject it on the ground that it is repetitious. But it is not repetitious, depending on what one understands by "repetition." Fulton J. Sheen has this story for those who describe the rosary as repetitious.

> A woman came one evening after instruction to see me. She said, "I would never become a Catholic. You say the same words in the Rosary over and over again, and anyone who repeats the same words is never sincere. I would never believe anyone who repeated his words, and neither would God." I asked her who the man with her was. She said he was her fiancé. I asked, "Does he love you?"

"Certainly he does." "But how do you know?" "He told me." "What did he say?" "He said, 'I love you.'" "When did he tell you last?" "He said it an hour ago." "Did he tell you before?" "Yes, last night." "What did he say?" "I love you." "But never before?" "He tells me every night." Then I told her, "Do not believe him. He is repeating; he is not sincere."

Sheen then added, "The beautiful truth is that there is no repetition in 'I love you.' Because there is a new moment of time, another point in space, the words do not mean the same as they did at another time or space."[42]

Devotion to the Angels and the Saints

Catholics are criticized for their devotion to the angels and the saints. Non-Catholics do not understand why they should ask the angels or the saints to intercede for them since Jesus is the only mediator between God and man. However, when the place of the angels and saints in our lives as Christians is properly understood, intercessors will appreciate them as great partners in their intercessory mission. The following biblical passage will help us understand that devotion to the angels and saints is an arrow in the quiver of an intercessor.

> But you have come to Mount Zion and to the city of the living God, the heavenly Jerusalem, and to innumerable angels in festal gathering, and to the assembly of the first-born who are enrolled in heaven, and to a judge who is

---

[42] Fulton J. Sheen, *The World's First Love: Mary, Mother of God* (San Francisco: Ignatius Press, 2010), p. 208.

> God of all, and to the spirits of just men made perfect,
> and to Jesus, the mediator of a new covenant, and to the
> sprinkled blood that speaks more graciously than the
> blood of Abel. (Heb. 12:22–24)

This passage highlights the brotherhood of all the children of God on earth and in heaven. In every act of Christian worship, we meet with an uncountable number of angels and the saints (the spirits of the righteous made perfect). We all come to Jesus, who is the Mediator of the new covenant. Bodily death does not create any barrier to this holy fraternity. Believers are not in reality separated from one another by corporeal death, time, or space. Thus, we remain with our fellow believers, who have gone before us and have been made perfect by the Lord they served here on earth. We are forever with them one family of God. Thus, St. Paul says, "Whether we live or whether we die, we are the Lord's" (Rom. 14:8). Only spiritual death, which results from sin, can separate us temporarily or permanently, as the case may be. The only difference between believers who are still here on earth and the saints in heaven is that while we live in time and space, they live in eternity, and whereas we are imperfect, they have been made perfect. And just as our fellowship with God is ageless, so our comradeship with our victorious brothers and sisters does not end.

Considering the fact that we belong to the same family of God and accordingly become brothers and sisters, the Bible admonishes us to pray for one another and bear each other's burdens (see James 5:16; Gal. 6:2). Those who have gone before us to join the glory above cannot stop praying for their brothers and sisters, whom they left behind here on earth, just because they have gone into eternity. After all, they are not dead. Death is not a passage into oblivion but a passing on into life. One should not think that those who have died are gone forever and have no communion with us anymore. If this were the case, why does the Bible say that we have come with them and the holy angels to Jesus at the sacred festival? If there were nothing we still share in common, why should they gather at every divine assembly with us? According to the *Cambridge Bible Commentary*, the passage above describes "'the Communion of the Saints above and the Church below' with myriads of Angels united in a festal throng."[43] We cannot perceive what happens in the spiritual realm except by faith, which is why we sometimes have difficulty believing in our everlasting communion with them. But we must remember that a believer lives by faith and not by sight.

Now, if we can request prayers from brothers and sisters we see, what is odd about requesting prayers from brothers and sisters we can see only with the eyes of faith? If Ogechi and Markus, who are fellow Christians here and now, can pray for us at our request, Saint Peter and Blessed Michael Iwene Tansi, as well as our saintly parents and relatives, who have been translated into glory (made perfect), can equally pray for us. But because we do not know who has been made perfect by the Master after transition from this earthly realm and therefore should be asked to intercede for us, we depend on the wisdom of the Church (which tells us who officially qualifies as a saint) to help us in our prayers.[44]

---

[43] *Cambridge Bible Commentary*, Commentary on Hebrews 12, Bible Hub, http://biblehub.com/commentaries/cambridge/hebrews/12.htm.

[44] This does not mean that only those beatified or canonized by the Church belong to this group of the spirits of the just, made perfect. There are millions of saints, who have not been

On another note, spiritual levels are not the same. There are hierarchies of nearness to God. Just as all angels do not possess equal status, all saints do not share equal status, and among human beings, too, there are different levels of nearness to God. This is the reason we believe that some people are more spiritually disposed and therefore spiritually higher than others, and we tend to request prayers more from them than we do from others. This is comparable to hiring an attorney. Nobody wants to hire an attorney who is not known for winning cases or whose profession has become moribund. We act in the same way when we request prayers from others. The logic behind this natural understanding is our belief that the prayer of a righteous man has great power in its effects (James 5:16).

But who among us is more righteous than the angels and the saints, whom we encounter as often as we meet at the "joyful assembly"? The answer to this is implied in the words of the Master concerning John the Baptist: "Truly, I say to you, among those born of women there has risen no one greater than John the Baptist; yet he who is least in the kingdom of heaven is greater than he" (Matt. 11:11). It is therefore evident that the prayer of the angels and our brothers and sisters already "made perfect" can be more effective than our own.

This does not mean that our prayers are weak or that we should essentially depend on the angels and the saints for spiritual aid. We do not stop praying simply because we've asked others to put us in their prayers. No attorney can defend his client without the client's cooperation. The angels and the saints need our

---

recognized by the Church formally as having already been made perfect. It is for this reason that the Church celebrates All Saints' Day on November 1 every year.

commitment to prayer to help us. Our prayers must principally be directed to God through Jesus. For our prayers are equally effective, when we pray rightly. The angels and the saints only support our prayers by telling God also about us and our petitions. They surely can obtain favors for us from God. Many experiences and testimonies of Christians give credence to their positive contributions in our lives here on earth. God can also use them as our spiritual companions in our earthly struggles.

One day, a young man came to a priest and narrated how he was experiencing incessant attacks every night in his dreams. He would not come out of such sleeps without physical wounds sustained during his nightmare fights. The priest knew that he was experiencing a demonic oppression. The priest prayed for him, but the problem persisted. One early morning, the man met the priest after his morning Mass and told him that an unknown hefty man had slapped him in a dream. He showed him his cheek with four long finger marks, indicating that his story was not a mere fairy tale or his dream an ordinary one. The priest prayed for the man again and then decided to put around his neck the medal of the then-Blessed Padre Pio of Pietrelcina. The next morning the young man ran frantically to the priest and asked him: "Who is this man you hung on my neck? Do his hands bleed?" The priest was stunned. The man had never heard of this saint, and the priest had not told him that the saint whose medal he had given him was a stigmatist. So, how did the man know that he had bleeding hands?

The priest then asked him what happened, and he recounted how giant scorpions surrounded him in his nightmare. They were fast approaching him with merciless ferocity while a group of stern-looking men stood by, jeering at his helplessness. "It was so lucid, Father. I saw him," he said. "He appeared from my neck with profusely bleeding hands. He picked up a blazing sword," he said flustered, "and destroyed the scorpions. He then chased the young men away. I got up immediately, thinking he was in my room, but I could not find him. I held my medal up from my neck and looked at it closely, and it was exactly the picture of the man who fought for me," he concluded, heaving a sigh of sweet relief. "Father, who is he?" He peered into the eyes of the priest with probing interest.

This is one out of myriads of such services angels and saints render to us but, of course, at the behest of the Master. The power of intercession of heavenly friends, however, gives the bidding a different force. Recourse to the angels or saints can be very helpful to intercessors. When they are invoked, they can persuade the Master, when necessary, to permit them to render some help. The Lord, in His love, can equip them to help us, for our sake and for His glory. They can also present our requests with better arguments and make them more appealing to the Lord and, in this way, may obtain favors for us. It is recommended, therefore, that intercessors should have some friends from the assembly above who can help push their cause into favor. It should be noted that it is the angels who offer the prayers of believers through incense to God (see Rev. 5:8) even though Jesus is undoubtedly the only Mediator between God and man.

Chapter 5

The Strike of the Serpent and the Blessed Assurance

We have discussed above that the mission of an intercessor, just like that of every Christian, is a spiritual military engagement. This militarism started a very long time ago. We are born into it and must fight our way to salvation. The Second Vatican Council Fathers strongly noted that the whole of human history has been the story of this combat with the powers of evil stretching from the very dawn of history until the last day.[45] Recall that when the war that broke out in heaven ended, the ancient serpent and his angels were defeated and hence lost their place in heaven. John the Evangelist reported: "And the great dragon was thrown down, that ancient serpent, who is called the Devil and Satan, the deceiver of the whole world — he was thrown down to the earth, and his angels were thrown down with him" (Rev. 12:9).

It was this serpent that found Eve in the garden and deceived her and Adam and instigated their rebellion against God. The consequence of this evil enticement and human disobedience

---

[45] Second Vatican Council, Pastoral Constitution on the Church in the Modern World *Gaudium et spes* (December 7, 1965), no. 37.

was the declaration of war by God between the woman and the serpent and between the seed of the woman and the seed of the serpent: "I will put enmity between you and the woman, and between your seed and her seed; He shall bruise your head, and you shall bruise His heel" (Gen. 3:15). According to the *Cambridge Bible Commentary*:

> The hostility between the serpent and the woman, between the serpent's seed and the woman's seed, typifies the unending conflict between all that represents the forces of evil on the one hand, and all that represents the true and high destiny of mankind on the other. Upon this antagonism Jehovah has, as it were, set His seal from the very beginning. He has ordained it. There must be war between every form of evil and the children of man.

This hostility is a very fierce one. The Septuagint Bible uses the Latin word *inimicitas* for *enmity* to denote that the conflict is like a blood feud. However, the Lord gave the woman and her seed an edge over the serpent and its seed in this warfare when he declared to the serpent: "He shall bruise your head, and you shall bruise his heel." Though the seed of the woman has the power of crushing the head of the serpent, he is not completely immune to the attacks of the serpent. It can venomously strike his heel. The serpentine poison injected through this strike can sometimes be life threatening. Inasmuch as every believer, as also the seed of the woman, is engaged in this war and, as such, exposed to danger, an intercessor, who is more likely in the first line of battle, is more exposed to the attacks of the enemy. He should therefore beware of the dangers necessitated by his mission.

The Strike of the Serpent and the Blessed Assurance

Hazards in the Spiritual Warfare of Intercession

Since no war is without dangers, the warfare of intercession has its own hazards, too. The war of intercession is a spiritual war, and spiritual warfare is far more complex, fiercer, and dangerous than any material warfare one can think of. Nobody should expect to win such a sophisticated war without possessing an adequate knowledge of the art of spiritual warfare and possessing the necessary supernatural weapons of war.

Spiritual warfare means a war against spiritual entities of organized wickedness, as already explained. They are invisible to the intercessor, but the intercessor is visible to them. They are much more acquainted with spiritual matters than the intercessor and can better interpret the conditions of war, and they know to a larger extent what to expect and how to neutralize their enemies. Although they do not have the power to read minds, they can intelligently interpret the state of mind of their combatants through existing visible signs. For this reason, an intercessor must not underestimate the strength of this diabolical army.

As we said earlier, intercession involves, among other things, wading into the territory of the enemy for a rescue mission. It is a very hazardous venture to cross the battle line, much less to go into the dungeon of the enemy to free his prisoners. Yet no one can truly be an intercessor without being able to do this.

Now, no one will believe that a lion will not roar when its den is invaded. "For every action there must be a reaction" is not only a law in physics; it is also a law in metaphysics. When an intercessor exerts power by the force of his supplications, there will arise negative spiritual powers to counter him: the enemy seeks in this encounter the source of this power that opposes him and goes all out to destroy it.

The Art of Spiritual Warfare

The Lord informed us that the enemy has a tripartite mission: to steal, to kill, and to destroy (see John 10:10). This is the mission he has vowed to accomplish. Anybody therefore, who stands in his way, is bound to receive his venom. This is when the battle begins in earnest. There are chances that an intercessor might be wounded in this battle or even be killed. It is for this reason that he must carefully learn the art of spiritual warfare so that, as St. Paul said, he may be able to withstand the enemy in the evil day, and having done all, to remain standing (see Eph. 6:13).

It must be underlined that the Lord did not promise that an intercessor would go through enemy territory unscathed. His words are rather that the serpent will strike our heel and we will, in turn, crush its head (Gen. 3:15). This is an indication that here the hard way is the only way. There is no other way to attain heaven or take people to heaven than to engage in this warfare. It is like picking treasure from a crucible. Yet there is a promise of victory in this statement of the Master, if we fight on the Lord's side and according to His military orders. Every intercessor must therefore always be ready to extinguish all the flaming arrows of the evil one (Eph. 6:16) and be conscious of the possible retaliation of the enemy following his intercessory exploits.

The devil is intelligent and cunning. He is equally patient. He can postpone his attacks till the time the intercessor lays down his guard. He knows when best to attack. He also knows where and when it hurts most. He surely knows how to precipitate troubles and prepare pains for his enemies. He might accordingly orchestrate some forms of organized and intelligent but diabolical attacks intended to frustrate an intercessor or a Christian and make him abandon his mission. He might decide to go directly or indirectly. He might, for instance, scheme to gather people and things that will continue to embitter one's disposition so that the intercessor's prayer will become merely routine, if he prays at all. His plan might even be to use these circumstances cunningly to push the intercessor into taking actions that would make him guilty before the divine council and blunt his spiritual weapons. He is an accuser and works hard to create circumstances for accusations. And he knows when best to do this.

This was what he sought when he came to Jesus after His forty-day fast. When he failed, he did not abandon his mission. No, he waited for an opportune moment (Luke 4:13). But the Master knew that and was prepared for the enemy's retaliation. Jesus was a major target because He came to undo the works of the evil one (1 John 3:8). That is equally the mission of an intercessor in his own capacity, and for this reason he is also a target. Many opportune moments, as the devil expected, presented themselves for him to launch his attacks during the ministry of Jesus. His intention was to stop the mission at all costs. One opportunity created itself after Jesus preached in the synagogue and condemned the unbelief of the Jews:

> Truly, I say to you, no prophet is acceptable in his own country. But in truth, I tell you, there were many widows in Israel in the days of Elijah, when the heaven was shut up three years and six months, when there came a great famine over all the land; and Elijah was sent to none of them but only to Zarephath, in the land of Sidon, to a woman who was a widow. And there were many lepers in Israel in the time of the prophet Elisha; and none of them was cleansed, but only Naaman the Syrian. (Luke 4:24–27)

The Art of Spiritual Warfare

When the people heard this, all in the synagogue were furious. They got up, drove Him out of town, and took Him to the brow of the hill on which the town was built, in order to throw Him off the cliff. This was at the instigation of the enemy, because the message of Christ itself did not warrant the overreaction of the Jews. The enemy had two alternative plans with this instigation: to make them throw Him off the cliff and kill Him or to force Jesus to become equally furious and when drenched with anger to fight back, giving the devil the opportunity to do evil. Either of the two would have aborted His mission. That was the ultimate aim of the devil. But Jesus knew better than to fall into the trap. He remained calm and wise, and, helped by grace, walked through the crowd and went on His way. A direct attack from the enemy followed the strong penitential message Jesus delivered in the synagogue.

Indirect attacks are a bit more complex than direct attacks. The enemy might decide to pick on one's family, parents, siblings, children, spouse, relations, business, job, or whoever and whatever one considers very dear. Thus, an intercessor must present all these before the Lord always and pray for His protection.

Now, if the devil is not to outdo an intercessor in cunning, the intercessor must understand his tricks and even predict his next moves. Any carelessness on the side of the intercessor may be very dangerous. No soldier can afford to be careless or carefree on the battlefield. The general life of an intercessor is fragile and must be handled as such. He cannot trifle with his sanctity, which is the bedrock of his security. A lapse in righteousness is a blow that is enough to crack the walls of defense of an intercessor, which can make him very vulnerable. The same thing can happen when an intercessor pitches his tent on the platform of doubt and distrusts the Master, thereby making Him small in his sight, or when he becomes impatient and decides to shoot or retire for rest without receiving a command from the Lord of the armies. The devil, being a good and intelligent marksman, can exploit this opportunity without fail.

There was once an intercessor who accompanied a group of intercessors to a warfare, but ended up being possessed by one of the demons that was sent packing. It was later discovered that earlier that morning, he had a female visitor with whom he shared a passionate kiss and other impure acts. He presumed that this did not mean much and went to battle without confessing it or even repenting of it. Yet St. Paul warned, "Give no opportunity to the devil" (Eph. 4:27).

One other day an intercessor was going for fellowship after some heated quarrel with his wife in which he used words that are totally unbecoming of a Christian, not to speak of an intercessor. On his way, a little girl that was very fond of him did not run to greet him as usual but rather said to him, "You are black inside." That was enough warning to him from the Lord.

These instances could perhaps help us to understand what happened to the sons of Scheva in the Acts of the Apostles 19:11–20. It was not because they were not Christians that they suffered severe attacks from the demons they tried to cast out. It was rather because they were "black inside." They wanted to cast out the demons for selfish purposes. They were inflated with pride and wanted to show that they could be as powerful as the apostles. They were, in short, seeking cheap popularity, for sheer vanity. That was enough to make them "black inside."

An intercessor should always be vigilant. He should not take chances and must make sure that every door that should not be open is closed and that every door that should be open is not closed. St. Peter advises: "Be sober, be watchful. Your adversary the devil prowls around like a roaring lion, seeking someone to devour. Resist him, firm in your faith" (1 Pet. 5:8–9). This is an informed counsel from a combat-experienced general. The enemy is on the prowl to tear and to devour. Therefore, he must be watched carefully. An intercessor must know that any breathing space given him could prove disastrous. We take a lesson from the thicket of shrubs: "In the forest, one shrub latches on to another, entangling its neighbor with its thorns, the thicket slowly extending its impenetrable domain."[46] The alertness and security of an intercessor must remain as closely latched as that of the thicket of shrubs.

A little relapse of security could be fatal for an intercessor. A little carelessness can cost him much more than he can imagine. As an intercessor, one must not give the devil the chance to reinforce and attack successfully. If an intercessor engages the enemy, he should hold him crushed in the dust, and should be cognizant of the fact that the devil does not give up easily. Therefore, if he binds a demon, he should make sure he remains bound. Robert Green has these words of wisdom to offer: "A viper crushed beneath your foot but left alive, will rear up and bite you with a double dose of venom. An enemy that is left around is like a half-dead viper that you nursed back to health. Time makes the venom grow stronger."[47] If you decide to be an intercessor, or already are one, analyze carefully and drink in this wise ancient composition:

> Christian, seek not yet repose.
> Hear thy guardian angels say:

[46] Greene, *The 48 Laws of Power*, p. 55
[47] Ibid. p. 113.

"Thou art in the midst of foes:
'Watch and pray!'"

Principalities and powers,
Mustering their unseen array,
Wait for thine unguarded hours:
"Watch and pray!"

Gird thy heavenly armor on,
Wear it every night and day.
In ambush lurks the evil one:
"Watch and pray!"

Watch as if on that alone,
Hung the issue of the day;
Pray, that help may be sent down:
"Watch and pray!"

An intercessor faces great danger if he abandons his mission. Once one becomes an intercessor, one must remain an intercessor. When a soldier quits fighting at the heat of a battle and turns his back to run away, he kisses the dust. An intercessor is hence engaged in a fight to the finish. The soldier of the gospel, according to the Pauline context, is accordingly equipped. Note that only his front, like the ancient Roman soldier, is protected. His rear is unprotected. This is intentional. An ancient Roman soldier is intended to move only frontward. Since his back is unprotected, he is forced to fight to the finish. A soldier of Christ is prepared in the same way. He too cannot abandon the fight and run away without tragic consequences. An intercessor who at any time abandons his intercessory mission after having been part of this ministry that destroys evil kingdoms, snatches away captives, and populates heaven to the glory of the Master, can expect no mercy from the enemy, if he plays into his hands. Thus, the Lord said: "Be faithful unto death, and I will give you the crown of life" (Rev. 2:10).

We must recall that one need not be a member of a particular intercessory team to become part of the ministry of intercession. One can function like Daniel by operating from a private room but uniting spiritually with other intercessors throughout the universe. Whichever one, community or private intercession, you choose to operate with, you must remain consistent and fight to the finish.

Do Not Be Afraid

Should all this tale of the hazards involved in the ministry of intercession scare you from answering the call to become an intercessor? The information above is meant only to alert an intercessor or prepare a prospective intercessor and not to scare you. This is why the intercessory ministry needs courageous men and women of God. Indeed, intercession has never been a ministry for cowards and never will be. This is because right from the time of John the Baptist, the kingdom of God has suffered violence and only men of violence can take it back by storm (see Matt. 11:12).

Intercessors are on a rescue mission. To rescue captives, they must wade into the territory of the enemy and snatch his captives. For "even the captives of the mighty shall be taken, and the prey of the tyrant be rescued" (Isa. 49:25). Intercessors are even expected to make the captor captive in the process. Only those who are truly begotten by the Lion of the tribe of Judah and therefore possess a lion's spirit can do this. They take after their Father and commander.

The powers and the would-be-exploits of the Lion of Judah were strongly noted in the prophecy of Jacob as he blessed his children: "Judah, your brothers shall praise you; your hand shall be on the neck of your enemies; your father's sons shall bow down before you. Judah is a lion's whelp; from the prey, my son, you have gone up. He stooped down, he couched as a lion, and as a lioness; who dares rouse him up?" (Gen. 49:8–9). Jesus came from the tribe of Judah and is indeed the real figure referred to in this passage, for the prophecy continued thus: "The scepter shall not depart from Judah, nor the ruler's staff from between his feet, until He comes to whom it belongs; and to Him shall be the obedience of the peoples" (Gen. 49:10). Jesus came, waged a great battle against the enemy like the king of the jungle, the lion, and took captivity captive (see Ps. 68:18; Eph. 4:8). This scenario was carefully recorded in the Gospel of Matthew, in the events that followed the Crucifixion and death of Christ:

> And Jesus cried again with a loud voice and yielded up His spirit. And behold, the curtain of the temple was torn in two, from top to bottom; and the earth shook, and the rocks were split; the tombs also were opened, and many bodies of the saints who had fallen asleep were raised, and coming out of the tombs after His resurrection they went into the holy city and appeared to many. (Matt. 27:50–53)

This clearly depicts the rumbling of war, which the Man of War carried to the underworld when it was thought that He was dead. The curtain of the temple, which had signified the division be-tween God and man, was torn in two from top to bottom, signi-fying that there is no more objective barrier between God and humanity. God and man have been reconciled. "The earth shook, the rocks split, and the tombs broke open," indicating that a rampaging war of liberation of captives was under way. Though Jesus was dead in the flesh, in the spirit He was alive (see 1 Pet. 3:18), waging war in the underworld and liberating captives. He destroyed the power of the tomb, the power of death, and set captives free. Many of the liberated "came out of the tombs after Jesus' resurrection and went into the holy city and appeared to many people."

When He had taken all captives away and wrecked the kingdom of the captor, the Father raised Him from the dead. It was then that He charged the disciples to go on doing the same thing He had done: "All authority in heaven and on earth has been given to me. Go therefore and make disciples of all nations" (Matt. 28:18–19). An intercessor must take note of this background and do away with any form of fear. He must remember the Master's instruction to Joshua, "be strong and courageous" (Josh. 1:6, NIV).

The Lord does not send without providing for the sent. He cannot send a messenger without going before him. He is always part of the missions that originate from Him. He thus has a lot of protection and other provisions for His servants. Consider the encounter of the prophet Elisha with the Syrian army.

When Elisha frustrated the Syrian army through his prophetic ministry, the Syrian king vowed to kill him. He consequently sent his army to go and arrest Elisha. Elisha himself was well acquainted with the promise of the Master through his servant Moses: "The Lord will cause your enemies who rise against you to be defeated before you; they shall come out against you one way, and flee before you seven ways" (Deut. 28:7); and with the fact that He who is in us is greater than he who is in the world (see 1 John 4:4). He therefore entertained no flicker of fear as the mighty Syrian army set out to undo him. But his servant Gehazi, who was still blind in spiritual matters, was melting in fear. So, the man of God prayed, "O Lord, I pray thee, open his eyes that he may see." The Lord answered his petition and opened the eyes of Gehazi. "So, the Lord opened the eyes of the young man, and he saw; and behold, the mountain was full of horses and chariots of fire round about Elisha" (2 Kings 6:17).

An intercessor should realize that those called by the name of the Lord and who are truly of God have such a divine protection that is invisible and invincible. They are the apple of the Lord's eye (Zech. 2:8), and the Master has threatened that He will command the slaves of whosoever dares to touch them to plunder their masters. To give them a maximum security, the Lord has erected a great wall of fire around them and made himself the glory within them (see Zech. 2:5). There is no doubt that His decree that no weapon fashioned against them will prosper (see Isa. 54:17) is forever active and effective. He equally made His name a fortified tower into which the righteous can run and get protected (see Prov. 18:10). There are many more such security outfits the Master has designed for His ministers, messengers, and servants. Why then should anybody be afraid? We have weapons of attack and weapons of defense and these weapons of warfare "are not worldly but have divine power to destroy strongholds" (2 Cor. 10:4). Why then should we not confidently go to war?

In warfare, it is an intelligent strategy to be acquainted with the tricks and modes of operation of the enemy. Being conversant with the nature of his weapons of war will be of a great advantage toward neutralizing the enemy's attacks even before the attacks are launched.

Now, the strongest weapon of the evil one is fear. This four-lettered word has destroyed many soldiers of the Master and incapacitated many of His human armies. Many ministers of the Lord have fallen because of this word *fear*. It is a monster that should never be allowed to rear its ugly head. Whenever it is allowed to strike with success, it tears down the walls of faith. When the rampart of faith collapses, doubts and confusion set in. One begins to live by sight and judge matters completely falsely. Prayer then becomes cold, disjointed, and feeble because the heart that prays has been invaded by fear. Accordingly, there is no more conviction in the heart that prays and, as such, no more force to transport prayers to the divine presence. An intercessor consequently becomes helplessly vulnerable. When the devil has successfully set up this disastrous state of affairs, he begins his tripartite job of stealing, killing, and destroying. It is for this reason that an intercessor must know that fear is a foe.

It is not therefore difficult to discover why Jesus always warned His apostles and disciples not to be afraid. At each moment of gathering tension He would say, "Do not be afraid." To counter fear and highlight its caustic effect, He would often tell them, "take courage"; "peace be with you" — so much so that this exhortation became His first gift to them when He rose from the dead. The Church appreciates this wonderful gift of serenity and equanimity that combats fear and prays at every Eucharistic sacrifice, "Deliver us from evil" and the participants in the sacrifice would pray for peace and wish each other the peace of Christ that the world cannot give.

No matter the nature of your storm, therefore, you must not allow fear to control your destiny. A wise man prayed: "God, grant me the serenity to accept the things I cannot change, courage to change the things I can, and wisdom to know the difference." Serenity is what we need to stand in battle. The psalmist knows the danger of fear and loss of equanimity. He therefore stands always very firm against it: "The Lord is my light and my salvation; whom shall I fear? The Lord is the stronghold of my life; of whom shall I be afraid? When evildoers assail me, uttering slanders against me, my adversaries, and foes, they shall stumble and fall. Though a host encamp against me, my heart shall not fear; though war arise against me, yet I will be confident" (Ps. 27:1–3).

In another place he confidently sings: "God is our refuge and strength, a very present help in trouble. Therefore, we will not fear though the earth should change, though the mountains shake in the heart of the sea; though its waters roar and foam, though the mountains tremble with its tumult. The Lord of hosts is with us; the God of Jacob is our refuge" (Ps. 46:1–3, 7).

One of the greatest psalms that offers confidence and gives assurance is Psalm 23. He who carefully digests its contents can stand up against fear, knowing that there is no ground whatsoever to be afraid:

> The Lord is my shepherd, I shall not want;
> He makes me lie down in green pastures.
> He leads me beside still waters; He restores my soul.
> He leads me in paths of righteousness for His name's sake.
> Even though I walk through the valley of the shadow of
>   death,
> I fear no evil; for thou art with me;
> thy rod and thy staff, they comfort me.
> Thou preparest a table before me
> in the presence of my enemies;
> thou anointest my head with oil, my cup overflows.
> Surely goodness and mercy shall follow me all the days of
>   my life;
> and I shall dwell in the house of the Lord for ever.

The Art of Spiritual Warfare

The men and women of God, who have gone before us, succeeded because they knew, like St. Paul, that we are more than conquerors through Him who loves us (cf. Rom. 8:37).

Therefore, do not fear.

Epilogue

In Matthew 6:9–15, Jesus teaches His disciples how to pray. This prayer became what we have today as the Lord's Prayer. In verse 10, we pray: "Your kingdom come, Your will be done on earth as it is in heaven" (NIV). This kingdom is explained by Barclay as the society upon earth where God's will is perfectly done, as it is done in heaven. But since the world is very far from being a place where God's will is perfectly and universally done, and since nothing on earth can ever be perfect, he explained: "The consummation of the kingdom is still in the future and is still something for which we must pray."

In the Lord's Prayer, therefore, Jesus invites us to pray for the consummation of the kingdom of God. He exhorts us to ask for this kingdom to be established, for it to materialize and be perfected, and for its consummation not to be frustrated by the forces of evil. This is our role in the establishment of the kingdom of God.

One might ask: Why did Jesus ask us to do this? Why does God need our prayers to make His kingdom come? What does He need from us that He cannot provide himself to establish His kingdom? Surely, He is omnipotent and can personally accomplish whatever He wills. So why then can He not make His kingdom come without involving us? He is equally omniscient and, no doubt, knows what to do for His kingdom to be consummated. What then does He need us for?

That God invites us to collaborate with Him in the building of His kingdom does not mean that He cannot do without us or that He is not almighty and can surely accomplish whatever interests Him. God is, rather, a Father par excellence. He is very loving and dear to His children. He calls His "children" those He adopted through the Cross of Christ His Son, who shares the same essence with Him. Thus, John the evangelist testifies: "See what love the Father has given us, that we should be called children of God; and so we are" (1 John 3:1). Being His special workmanship (Eph. 2:10) and reflecting His image and glory, He regards his children very highly, as invaluable treasures. St. Peter expresses this awesome status when He writes: "But you are a chosen race, a royal priesthood, a holy nation, God's own people" (1 Pet. 2:9).

Just as any responsible father would like to see himself in his children, see them mature and develop a personality with character, and then proudly entrust them with responsibilities, so God wants to take pride in His own children by seeing them reflect Him. Thus, since He is still working (see John 5:17), He would not expect His children to be idling away instead of being busy with their Father in His workshop. Now, His entire work is geared toward the making of His kingdom. He thus wants His children to be part of this project as an honor due to children from a loving and responsible Father. With this honor He makes them co-workers with Him in the shaping and consummation of His kingdom.

This is not because He is unable to do it alone. He simply wants the children to have the fulfilment of being children in His house and enjoy their entitlements (their sonship). In this way

He expresses His palpable confidence and trust in His adopted children by inviting them to be His collaborators. He wants them to have the joy and pride of children working together with their father. Considering the fact that we, the children, are unworthy to receive this enviable gesture from the Master, we must then understand that this is an awesome privilege the Father has bestowed on us. Accordingly, the psalmist asks: "What is man that thou art mindful of him, and the son of man that thou dost care for him?" (Ps. 8:4).

The coming of the kingdom of God is the process of perfecting the will of God on earth as it is in heaven. A call to intercession is therefore a call to pray for God's kingdom to come, a call to intercede so that all structures of evil will collapse. It means a call to demolish everything that resists the perfecting of the will of God. An invitation to intercede is simply a call to participate in the building of the kingdom of God, a kingdom of truth and life, a kingdom of holiness and grace, a kingdom of justice, love, and peace. It is an invitation to exercise the awesome privilege of working with God, our Father, in the realization of His kingdom; a call to appropriate our noble and privileged role in tearing down the kingdom of wickedness while erecting the kingdom of our Father. When we intercede for our decaying world, we are fulfilling this mission. When we pray for lost souls and groan passionately for perishing souls, we are enhancing the consummation of the kingdom of God. For any evil structure we undo through our intercessions and our other Christian works, we further the coming of the Lord's kingdom.

Bibliography

Amorth, Gabriele. *An Exorcist Explains the Demonic: The Antics of Satan and His Army of Fallen Angels.* Manchester: Sophia Institute Press, 2016.

———. *An Exorcist: More Stories.* Translated by Nicholeta V. McKenzie. San Francisco: Ignatius Press, 2002.

Aquinas, Father. *The Holy Rosary.* New Mexico: Kingship of Christ, n.d.

Archimedes of Syracuse, *The Library of History of Diodorus Siculus, Fragments of Book XXVI.* Translated by F. R. Walton. In Loeb Classical Library (1957), vol. XI.

Aquinas, Thomas. *Summa Theologiae* I, q. 108.

Barclay, W. *The Daily Study Bible.* Vol. 2. Bangalore: Theological Pub., 1994.

Benson, Joseph. *Benson's Bible Commentary.* Bible Hub. http://biblehub.com/commentaries/benson/.

Berkeley, James D. "Burning Out, Rusting Out, or Holding Out?" *Christianity Today* (Winter 1983). http://www.christianitytoday.com/pastors/1983/winter/83l1036.html.

Cambridge Bible Commentary. Bible Hub. http://biblehub.com/commentaries/cambridge/.

The Catholic Encyclopedia. New York: Robert Appleton, 1907. New Advent, http://www.newadvent.org/cathen/.

Donnelly, Nick. "Freemason Service at England's Mother Church on Same Day as Consecration to Our Lady." Church Militant, February 17, 2017. https://www.churchmilitant.com/news/article/freemason-service-at-englands-mother-church-on-same-day-as-consecration-to.

"Fable of the Eagle and the Chicken." In Jamie Glenn, *Walk Tall, You're A Daughter of God*. Posted on Life Lessons, September 25, 2009. https://lifelessons4u.wordpress.com/tag/the-eagle-who-thought-he-was-a-chicken/.

"Famous Rosary Miracles." Miraculous Rosary. http://miraculousrosary.blogspot.com/p/famous-rosary-miracles.html.

Greene, Robert. *The 48 Laws of Power*. London: Profile Books, 2000.

Gregory the Great, *Homiliae xxxiv* in *Evangelia*.

Hornby, A. S. *Advanced Learner's Dictionary*. Edited by Sally Wehmeier. Oxford: Oxford University Press, 2012.

Ignatius of Antioch. *Letter to the Romans*. In *Early Christian Writings*, vol. 2. Translated by Andrew Louth. New York: Penguin, 1987.

Jasper, Karl. *The Future of Mankind*. Translated by E. B. Ashton. Chicago: University of Chicago Press, 1963.

Leo XIII. *On the Sect of the Freemasons*. London: Burns and Oates, 1884.

Bibliography

Ochiagha, Gregory O. *Friendship*. Snaps Press, 2003.

Paul VI. "Homily for the Canonization of the Ugandan Martyrs." In *The Liturgy of the Hours*, vol. II, Feast of Charles Lwanga and His companions.

———. Homily, June 29, 1972.

"Prayer Worked Miracles in the Philippines." FrTommyLane. com. http://www.frtommylane.com/stories/prayer/miracle_in_the_philipines.htm.

Saunders, William. "The History of the Rosary." EWTN. https://www.ewtn.com/library/ANSWERS/ROSARYHS.HTM.

Sheen, Fulton J. *In the Fullness of Time: Christ-Centered Wisdom for the Third Millennium*. Edited by Patricia A. Kossmann. Liguori, MS: Liguori/Triumph, 1999.

———. *The World's First Love: Mary, Mother of God*. San Francisco: Ignatius Press, 1952.

Tardif, Emiliano, and Jose H. Prado Flores. *Jesus Lebt*. Münsterschwarzach: Vier-Türme-Verlag, 1988.

Tertullian, *The Apology of Tertullian*. Translated by W. M. Reeve. London: Griffith, Farran, 1889.

Wakefield, R. "A Passion for Souls." *Higher Way Magazine* 93.

About the Author

Venatius Chukwudum Oforka is a Catholic priest ordained for the Catholic Diocese of Orlu, Nigeria. He has worked as a pastor in many parishes, both in Nigeria and abroad, and has consequently spent most of his more than twenty years of priestly life caring for souls. He has a master's degree in philosophy and theology and a doctoral degree in moral theology. He is the author of *The Bleeding Continent: How Africa Became Impoverished and Why It Remains Poor* and *Afro-Igbo Mmadụ and Thomas Aquinas's Imago Dei: An Intercultural Dialogue on Human Dignity.*

Sophia Institute

Sophia Institute is a nonprofit institution that seeks to nurture the spiritual, moral, and cultural life of souls and to spread the gospel of Christ in conformity with the authentic teachings of the Roman Catholic Church.

Sophia Institute Press fulfills this mission by offering translations, reprints, and new publications that afford readers a rich source of the enduring wisdom of mankind.

Sophia Institute also operates two popular online Catholic resources: CrisisMagazine.com and CatholicExchange.com.

Crisis Magazine provides insightful cultural analysis that arms readers with the arguments necessary for navigating the ideological and theological minefields of the day. *Catholic Exchange* provides world news from a Catholic perspective as well as daily devotionals and articles that will help you to grow in holiness and live a life consistent with the teachings of the Church.

In 2013, Sophia Institute launched Sophia Institute for Teachers to renew and rebuild Catholic culture through service to Catholic education. With the goal of nurturing the spiritual, moral, and cultural life of souls, and an abiding respect for the role and work of teachers, we strive to provide materials and programs that are at once enlightening to the mind and ennobling to the heart; faithful and complete, as well as useful and practical.

Sophia Institute gratefully recognizes the Solidarity Association for preserving and encouraging the growth of our apostolate over the course of many years. Without their generous and timely support, this book would not be in your hands.

www.SophiaInstitute.com
www.CatholicExchange.com
www.CrisisMagazine.com
www.SophiaInstituteforTeachers.org